MW00325630

Hidden Dangers

Mexico on the Brink of Disaster

Robert Joe Stout

SUNBURY PRESS

Mechanicsburg, Pennsylvania   USA

Published by Sunbury Press, Inc.
50 West Main Street, Suite A
Mechanicsburg, Pennsylvania 17055

www.sunburypress.com

Copyright © 2014 by Robert Joe Stout.
Cover copyright © 2014 by Sunbury Press, Inc.

Sunbury Press supports copyright. Copyright fuels creativity, encourages
diverse voices, promotes free speech, and creates a vibrant culture. Thank
you for buying an authorized edition of this book and for complying with
copyright laws by not reproducing, scanning, or distributing any part of it in
any form without permission. You are supporting writers and allowing
Sunbury Press to continue to publish books for every reader. For information
contact Sunbury Press, Inc., Subsidiary Rights Dept., 50-A W. Main St.,
Mechanicsburg, PA 17011 USA or legal@sunburypress.com.

For information about special discounts for bulk purchases, please contact
Sunbury Press Orders Dept. at (855) 338-8359 or orders@sunburypress.com.

To request one of our authors for speaking engagements or book signings,
please contact Sunbury Press Publicity Dept. at publicity@sunburypress.com.

ISBN: 978-1-62006-488-7 (Trade Paperback)
ISBN: 978-1-62006-489-4 (Mobipocket)
ISBN: 978-1-62006-490-0 (ePub)

FIRST SUNBURY PRESS EDITION: September 2014

Product of the United States of America
0 1 1 2 3 5 8 13 21 34 55

Set in Bookman Old Style
Designed by Lawrence Knorr
Cover by Amber Rendon
Edited by Janice Rhayem

Continue the Enlightenment!

Table of Contents

Preface

As a *gringo-Mexicano* writing *Hidden Dangers*, I have focused my research on personal experiences and interviews with a wide variety of people and upon contemporary commentary and criticism by Mexican writers and investigators. The intended viewpoint is neither pro-Mexican nor anti-Mexican, but a critical examination of situations between the two countries that are unresolved and potentially explosive. As a journalist, I have worked in both countries and published articles and essays about Mexico, its problems, people, achievements, and culture. Many of these were included in *The Blood of the Serpent: Mexican Lives* (Algora, 2003) and served as a basis for sections of *Why Immigrants Come to America* (Praeger, 2008). Many of the articles and essays published since the appearance of *Why Immigrants Come to America* incorporate or have been based on interviews and research accumulated for this book. They are noted in the bibliography.

Translations from articles and book sections and from personal interviews are mine. I have in all cases tried to be as exact as possible to the intent, both colloquial and academic, to what was written or said while presenting the material in grammatical English.

To facilitate indexing and alphabetical listings, I have inserted a hyphen between the two last names of Mexican citizens who identify themselves or who are identified professionally with both their father's and mother's surnames, i.e. "Miguel Concha-Malo" instead of "Miguel Concha Malo," Concha being the father's surname and Malo the mother's. This enables proper indexing in both languages.

INTRODUCTION

Former *New York Times* Mexico bureau chief, Alan Riding, entitled his 1985 best seller *Our Distant Neighbors.* Nearly a generation has passed since that writing, and the two countries remain as close—and as distant—as they were then. Mexico and the United States share a border that stretches for nearly 2,000 miles between the Pacific Ocean and the Gulf of Mexico. Deeply ingrained ethnic, economic, and political differences have escalated to the point that armed military forces have been deployed along the border by the leaders of both nations, some to combat a common enemy—the drug corporations—others to restrict immigration, smuggling, and money laundering.

Distant or not, Mexico is undergoing economic and political changes that lie like landmines ready to explode beneath the troubled and often discordant impulses of the two countries to satisfy their divergent social and political needs. These landmines include:

- Migration, legal and illegal, exacerbated by profound differences in earnings in the two countries and economic crises in both, a rapidly expanding labor pool and more aggressive deportation procedures on the part of U.S. Homeland Security;
- Intrusion by drug organizations into economic and political activities that include assassinations, payoffs, and escalating drug use in Mexico itself;
- Grass roots political movements opposed to globalization, centralized government, and unequal distribution of wealth that are being repressed, often violently, by Mexican political forces;
- Government and entrepreneurial corruption, including the failure to invest oil profits in infrastructure, debilitating the industry and putting most of the country's wealth in the hands of a few politically connected individuals;

1

- Environmental disasters and the collapse of self-sustaining agriculture that have created wastelands, polluted major waterways, and triggered rural-to-urban migrations.

Although Mexico's economy has produced some of the world's richest individuals, three-fourths of the population lives into poverty, much of it extreme. One-time self-sustaining coffee, corn, and poultry producing communities have become ghost towns. By 2010, twelve percent of Mexico's economically active population was working in the United States, an estimated seven million of them without legal documentation. The money they sent back to Mexico rose to US$23 billion a year in the mid-2000s, only slightly less than what was provided by oil exportations. The country's president, Felipe Calderón, sidled into office after obtaining slightly over one-third of the national vote in an election tainted by widespread allegations of fraud. Drug organization-connected murders became everyday events and unsolved feminicides numbered in the thousands.

Each of these "landmines" remains volatile in large part because the leaders and voters of the two countries lack mutually agreed upon definitions by which to identify the differences between their perceptions of the same political and cultural phenomena. They urge open border and free trade, but simultaneously militate extreme protectionism in matters of immigration and narcotics commerce. When politicians in the United States talk about the "immigration problem," the "drug problem," or the economy, they frame their concerns in an entirely different way from their Mexican counterparts. What many in the United States believe would resolve the immigration problem (eliminating the unauthorized entry of workers) would exacerbate situations in Mexico where residents would lose billions in remittances every year, and the country would be unable to provide work or incomes for those who don't migrate.

What would resolve the criminality of the drug cartels in Mexico (legalizing the export and transportation of marijuana and cocaine), could greatly increase the distribution of those illegal substances in the United

States. Similar differences affect private investment in Mexico's oil, gas, and electricity industries (much of the income derived would leave the country, and consumer costs would rise while benefiting the U.S. economy and possibility lowering energy costs for U.S. consumers), in agriculture and in the disposal of nuclear waste. It is my hope that this book will help define areas of discord and misunderstanding—"landmines"—and indicate alternatives that will help to diffuse them.

I must admit that my personal exposure to landmines is limited, but I have very vivid remembrances of crossing the border from Honduras into Nicaragua in 1987 during the civil conflict in the latter country. Because the bus from Choluteca, Honduras, unloaded passengers half a kilometer from the Honduran line, I had no choice but to walk to the other side to get transportation in Nicaragua to Somoto or Estelí.

Sentries manning the little *garita* inspected my papers after collecting a fee (which I had to pay in Honduran currency since I had no dollars), and suggested that I catch a ride with someone passing in a car or pickup, since the buses seldom ran on schedule and often didn't come all. But since it was a crisp, sunny January afternoon, I shouldered my two packs and strode along a fairly well-maintained road that I noticed was pockmarked here and there by what seemed to be bomb or shell craters.

Less than fifteen minutes into my commute, I heard a woman screech, "Get off the road! Get off the road!"

I shrugged, determined to ignore her—she had a wild look about her, what with broken teeth and gray streaked hair tied with a dirty bandana at her shoulder—but she continued to shout at me as she scrambled through the tangled shrubbery bordering the road. Finally I stopped, more curious than annoyed, and approached her.

"Get off the road you stupid fool!" she spit. "There are mines! Landmines!"

I got off the road. And I listened to her descriptions—and, later, descriptions by others—of deaths and amputations. When finally I caught a ride, I noticed that the driver, like the few other drivers we saw, avoided the road and bumped along rutted tracks grooved into the hillsides until we reached an unpaved and apparently unmined *carretera* several kilometers within Nicaragua.

"One needs to learn the territory," a Nicaraguan journalist warned me a few days later when I described the experience.

Good advice, I thought. Advice that every would-be diplomat should heed.

Although I've categorized these landmines (or minefields, if one wants a more extensive metaphor) under five headings, a certain amount of overlap exists among them. All are linked to the economy, to the political processes of the two countries, to the social dynamic in each of them, and to each country's separate and very different history. Since each topic has been treated by investigators and journalists as a singular issue, it seems appropriate to deal with them in separate sections despite this overlap. The book's conclusion summarizes how these sections converge and suggests ways to alleviate the dangers inherent in minefields.

During the first decade of the twenty-first century, the George W. Bush administration in particular, but also the Democratic Obama administration, devoted countless work hours and investigations to describe, affirm, and explain the dangers inherent in the rise of the drug cartels, to link unauthorized immigration with terrorism, to expound neoliberal economic doctrines, and to define the rise of popular movements as leftist, dangerous and criminal. They did so using terms like "democracy" and "our nation" as though defining a clearly visible concept just as their governing counterparts south of the border spoke of "*la patria*" and "*el pueblo*" as though they could physically be touched and photographed like the pyramids of Teotihuacan or the Statue of Liberty.

Since Bush's election in the year 2000 (and in Mexico the election of Vicente Fox and his "government of entrepreneurs, by entrepreneurs and for entrepreneurs" in July of that same year), many Mexicans' perception of the United States has soured dramatically. A majority of Mexican citizens that I talk to (I live in Oaxaca, in southern Mexico, but have traveled extensively throughout the country) blame their government for exacerbating the

4

poverty that drives workers northward—a government that since 1988 has forced over twenty million rural residents off the land they owned and increased dependence on costly imports of basic consumables, particularly corn. These same people are horrified by the increasing violence of drug trade, but angrily question the militarizing of cities and frontiers to curb the United States' exorbitant appetite for marijuana and cocaine.

They are unable to understand why the government of the United States refuses to limit its manufacturers from supplying the drug cartels and the Mexican military and militarized police with sophisticated armaments, many of which have been used to repress popular protests. They fail to understand why the U.S. government has militarized its persecution of undocumented immigrants even though jobs exist for them and employers willingly hire them.

Throughout Mexico, immigrating to the United States to work is considered honorable and necessary; those involved often are making great sacrifices to provide incomes for their families. In no way do they or their fellow citizens conceive them as criminals or terror threats. And although a huge percentage of them want what they perceive that most U.S. citizens have—a regular income, a house, a car, health care, educations for their children— they feel victimized by the political systems that exploit them.

In *What We Say Goes*, Noam Chomsky contrasts the economic status of the countries in Latin America and Africa most submissive to the dictates of the International Monetary Fund and World Bank with those that responded with minimum or negative reactions. Mexico, like others most deeply involved in borrowing and exporting raw materials at the cost of internal manufacturing and food production, suffered what Chomsky terms "catastrophic results" as a consequence of adhering to neo-liberal policies.[1]

Even during the flush years of José López Portillo's presidency (1976-1982) when the discovery of rich new oil reserves were pouring billions of dollars into federal coffers,

---

1   Noam Chomsky and David Barsamian, *In What We Say Goes*, (2007).

Petroleos Mexicanos (Pemex), the nationalized oil conglomerate, was spending more than it was taking in.[2] In order to become a major exporting nation, Mexico had to invest deeply in infrastructure—pipelines, refineries, drilling equipment, processing plants; to do so they borrowed heavily from the World Bank and refused to align themselves with OPEP in order to maximize exportation without having production limited. Even before the discovery of the new oil reserves, presidents since Gustavo Díaz Ordaz (1964-1970) emphasized raw material exports over investment in the country's manufacturing and agricultural capabilities and borrowing more than domestic production could repay. Each president in turn passed to his successor the flood of debt that eventually undermined the country's economic structure.

In November 2008, the U.S. Joint Forces Command issued a report describing Mexico and Pakistan as countries on the verge of collapse: "... [Mexico's] government, its politicians, police, and judicial infrastructure are all under sustained pressure by criminal gangs and drug cartels ... Any descent into chaos would demand an American response based on the serious implications for homeland security alone."[3]

Although the report accurately depicted situations along Mexico's frontier, it focused on headline-grabbing confrontations among drug cartels and assumed that military force was the answer to the violence, not a contributing cause. Kevin Kearney, in a column distributed online by *Narco News*, noted:

> Calderón's "war" on the long-standing and complex socio-economic problem of drug trafficking ... consisted of little more than a mass deployment of military units across the country ... nearly 50,000 troops—including federal police—have been deployed with an official mandate to use all necessary force ... the result is a much distorted

---

2   By 2010 Pemex's debt has soared to over fifty billion dollars despite the fact that it was exporting oil at 100 dollars per barrel and spending only five dollars a barrel on extraction.

3   "Joint Operating Environment," U.S. Joint Forces Command, November 25, 2008.

picture which portrays Mexico as a "wild west" environment where vicious drug dealers indiscriminately terrorize a helpless population that cries out for military assistance.[4]

Calderón and his predecessor in Mexico's presidency, Vicente Fox, adopted Bush administration rhetoric in committing the country to a "war on drugs" and pinpointing the "cartels" and "organized crime" as the enemy. But the cartels, per se, don't exist, although various federations responsible to specific entrepreneurs do. These organizations, or federations, incorporate legitimate and money laundering businesses, legal staffs, accountants, and a variety of semi-independent exporting and protection units, some of whose loyalties are questionable. They also include large numbers of police, military, and government employees, whose income from the drug transporters far exceeds what they receive from their legitimate professions.

Numerous high-ranking officials within Calderón's administration were singled out for their connections with individual *capos,* or drug lords. They included Public Safety Secretary Genero García-Luna, who journalist Anabel Hernández reported had built a mansion valued at over Mex$20 million, far more than he could finance from his cabinet salary.[5]

"García-Luna in charge of criminal investigations is like putting Marcial Maciel [the child molesting priest-founder of *Legionarios de Cristo*] in charge of an orphanage!" writer Ugo Codevilla snorted derisively during a 2009 presentation of his book *2006-2009, La Coyuntura Adversa.*[6]

PRI governors Armando León Bejarano, Jorge Carrillo-Olea, Tomas Yerington, and Mario Villanueva, PAN governors Sergio Estrada-Cajigal and Marco Adame-Castillo, high-ranking members of Mexico's top crime-

4   Kevin Kearney, *Narco News.*
5   Anabel Hernández, interviewed by Carmen Arestegui on "Reporte Indigo," January 13, 2012.
6   Ugo Codevilla, presentation of *Mèxico, 2006-2009, la coyuntura adversa* in Oaxaca, Oaxaca, January 23, 2009.

fighting agency, SIEDO (Sub-Prosecutor General of Special Investigations into Organized Crime), Army General Leopoldo Díaz-Pérez, and countless other elected and appointed officials were accused at various times of collaboration with individual drug organizations.

Proceso columnist Sabina Berman compared Calderón's "war on drugs" with the prohibition era in the United States.

Thanks to it being illegal, [during prohibition] the price of alcohol zoomed to stratospheric heights and its distribution and sale financed bands of gangsters to commit increasingly more destructive crimes ... their economic power permitted them to corrupt local and federal police until those agencies were totally incapacitated ... the real problem was not the alcohol but robbery, extortion and assassinations.[7]

By substituting the word "drugs" for "alcohol," one gets an accurate indictment of situations that worsened dramatically during the administrations of Vicente Fox and Felipe Calderón. The demand for imported narcotics in the United States, particularly cocaine, marijuana, and designer drugs, decreased only slightly during the first decade of the twenty-first century, while the majority of disappearances, extortions, and assassinations attributed to drug organization violence occurred south of the border.

The ruling powers of both countries chose to overlook statistics that indicated that forty years of persecuting dealers and importers hadn't lessened this demand for narcotics. To judge from the wealth the drug organizations have at their fingertips, the U.S. consumer base is enormous and there is nothing that more guns, more helicopters, and more troops can do has been able to diminish it.

Although Mexico's constitution limits use of the military to defending national boundaries, presidents prior to Fox and Calderón deployed troops to curtail domestic threats. Federal forces killed hundreds of striking railway workers in 1958 and a still undefined number of students and their

---

7   Sabina Berman, "La desventurada guerra de Elliot Ness," *Proceso,* April 5, 2009.

supporters were shot and their bodies secretly disposed of in 1968 during confrontations at Tlaltelolco in the Federal District.

Only Subcomandante Marcos's international notoriety prevented President Carlos Salinas de Gortari (1988-1994) from using full military force against the Zapatista uprising in the southern state of Chiapas in 1994; nevertheless, Salinas and his successors kept Zapatista communities surrounded by troops that made frequent forays into the autonomous villages, ostensibly searching for drugs. Journalist Hermann Bellinghausen, the author of a book describing the slaying of unarmed men, women, and children at Acteal, Chiapas, accused President Ernesto Zedillo (1994-2000) of "silent genocide" for a series of massacres by soldiers, police, and paramilitaries in the states of Chiapas and Guerrero. He insisted that official versions of putting down "impulsive eruptions" were intentionally planned repressions designed to deter protest movements.[8]

Zedillo, the third of three Institutional Revolutionary Party presidents with PhDs in economics from U.S. universities, was instrumental in the promulgation of the North American Free Trade Agreement (NAFTA), which Salinas de Gortari negotiated with U.S. President Bill Clinton. To create what Salinas de Gortari boasted would be Mexico's ascension into the "first world" the Mexican government reduced the landholding *campesino* population by nearly 30 million—one-third of the country's population.

The majority of displaced *campesinos* crowded into urban slums or migrated to the United States. Entrepreneurs taking advantage of NAFTA molded huge estates to produce export crops, replacing native growth with eucalyptus plantations for the production of pulpwood, and turning formerly small farms into denuded plains for cattle grazing. Former presidential candidate Andrés Manuel López Obrador in 2009 accused the "neo-liberal model," in the slightly over twenty years since its

---

8   Hermann Bellinghausen, "Miembros de la otra campaña, rehenes del poder en el penal Satiaguito," La Jornada, April 2, 2007. See also Bellinghausen, Acteal crimen de estado (2008).

inception, of creating "little islands of progress" surrounded by huge oceans of poverty.[9]

Vicente Fox, elected to the presidency in 2000, openly asserted his dedication to "a government of entrepreneurs, by entrepreneurs and for entrepreneurs." Before he left office in 2006, after what political cartoonist Josè Hernández (and many others) termed the *Sexenio Perdido* (the Lost Six Years), *Forbes* magazine listed several Mexican entrepreneurs on their list of the world's richest men, including Carlos Slim, who for a year replaced Bill Gates on the top rung of the ladder. But less than a year later, Mexico's Confederation of Business, Services and Tourism (Concanaco for its initials in Spanish), alarmed because internal production had fallen far below government estimates, warned the federal government that businesses and factories throughout Mexico had found it easier and more cost effective to import goods than produce them nationally.[10]

Many workers instrumental in the production of imported goods were Mexican *indocumentados* working in the United States. Accelerated detentions and deportations did not deter an estimated one million or more Mexicans from crossing the border every year during the 1990s and the first years of the twenty-first century. By 2006, remittances from the United States to Mexico by these workers reached US$24 billion, most of it sent weekly or monthly in US$100.00-$1,000.00 increments.

Mexican economists and various political leaders, including López Obrador, admitted that this migration brought stability to Mexico's economy, without which the country might have plunged into revolution. President Vicente Fox on various occasions called these migrant workers "national heroes" without mentioning that the remittances being received by Mexican communities enabled Mexico's federal government to curtail expenditures for social and educational programs. The PAN's (the National Action Party of presidents Fox and Calderón) much ballyhooed national health program,

---

9   Andrés Manuel López Obrador "El país desde abajo," *La Jornada,* March 10, 2009.
10   *La Jornada,* May 27, 2007.

Seguro Popular, foundered because there were no doctors for many rural clinics and almost all of the clinics lacked medicines. The few doctors assigned to them only could issue prescriptions for private pharmacies, which most rural residents could not afford to fill.

Nearly 60 percent of those living in Mexico's southern-most states, Oaxaca and Chiapas, depended upon remittances as their primary source of income. Percentages were almost as high in the northern states. Emigrant communities established in the United States often exceeded their communities of origin in Zacatecas, Durango, and Michoacán in population. The cities bordering the United States increased dramatically in size, but much of the available work was in *maquiladoras* (assembly plants), where workers, a high percentage of whom were women, earned barely enough to pay daily expenses.

Colonias populares (shantytowns) spread into the hills surrounding Tijuana and across the deserts of the states bordering Arizona and Texas. They included hundreds of thousands of unsuccessful emigrants who'd arrived penniless from the southern states of Mexico and from Guatemala, El Salvador, Nicaragua, and other countries in Central America. Border walls, sophisticated surveillance equipment, and workshop raids made emigrant life more hazardous and more difficult but did not deter the northward surge of under- and unemployed men, women, and teenagers.

From 1990 to 2010 an estimated two million young Mexicans tried to enter the Mexican work force every year. Despite the campaign promises of Zedillo, Fox, and Calderón, only a small percentage of these two million a year found permanent employment. By 2010, over half of the country's work force was involved in the informal economy, primarily as street vendors, day workers, and servants. Twelve percent of Mexican permanent jobholders lived and worked in the United States, nearly seven million of whom lacked proper authorization and survived in constant fear of being deported.

As prospects for employment diminished (or completely vanished), many young people entering the workforce sought to benefit themselves from the country's rapidly expanding—and most lucrative—business: the production and exportation of narcotics.

The lack of employment is one of the main challenges to national security, Mexican economist Rosa Albina-Garavito warned.[11] National University investigator Luis Astorga contended that the drug organizations had progressed past being criminal gangs, were employing market value tactics and psychology and hiring accountants, investors, lawyers, and computer experts, as well as armed bodyguards and hit men.[12]

Although many Mexican entrepreneurs moved their families and their centers of business to the United States, particularly south Texas, and surrounded themselves with bodyguards, they continued to support Calderón's "government of, by and for entrepreneurs." During the early part of the twenty-first century, international oil prices soared, providing Mexico's federal government with an immense amount of operating capital since the budgets on which expenditures were calculated were based on expectations of revenue at forty dollars a barrel for Mexican crude oil. The Calderón government chose to deal with part of this excess by rebating billions of dollars in tax payments to entrepreneurs as a stimulus to the economy.

Very little of it trickled down to Mexico's workers and even less to the *indigena* communities in Hidalgo, the Huasteca, and southern Mexico. The Pan Bimbo consortium, Maseca, Cemex, Televisa, Carlos Slim, and other Mexican entrepreneurs and financial groups invested heavily in expansion throughout Mexico, the United States, and Latin America. The world economic collapse in 2008 swept them with it despite assertions by Calderón and his finance minister, Agustín Carstens, that the country's economy was merely undergoing "a bit of a sniffle." By the time the sniffle had become full-blown pneumonia, many of those same entrepreneurs were demanding government relief.[13]

---

11 "El Artículo 123 y la deuda con las trabajadoras en el siglo XXI," forum in Mexico, D.F., January 28, 2011.
12 Luis Astorga, *El siglo de las drogas* (2005).

By January 2007, world oil prices had dropped drastically and Petróleos Mexicanos (Pemex), Mexico's nationalized oil industry, was unable to increase production after years of neglected maintenance and failures to update the infrastructure of processing and refining. During the preceding thirty years, the directors of Pemex and the heads of the oil workers union had become multibillionaires, and their financial dealings were never made available to the public. Although by definition Pemex "belongs to the people," as Mexico's president, Lázaro Cardenas, proclaimed when he nationalized the oil industry in 1938, the people had little or nothing to say about how the industry was run or where its money went.

PRI and PAN federal administrations adhered to the philosophy summarized by long-time political operative Carlos Hank-Gónzalez: "A politician who's poor is a poor politician."[14] Although corruption was acknowledged and often detailed after the fact, very seldom was any official convicted and sent to prison. (Exceptions included the former governor of Quintana Roo, Mario Villanueva, and Jorge Díaz-Serrano, the director of Pemex during the 1980s.) Mexican law granted immunity from prosecution for elected officials; they moved from post to post— governor to senator to *diputado* (congressman) taking with them an entourage of collaborators and assistants to fill sub-secretarial and other slots for which they had no qualifications except for the loyalty they'd shown their benefactor.

As happens in the United States (and in many other countries throughout the world), elected chiefs of state tend to choose persons they know and have worked with closely during their political careers for important positions in government. All too often these administrators and advisors contribute to, if not encourage, a chief executive's

---

13   "El Espasmo de los Chicago boys de Calderón," *Contralinea,* November 1, 2008.

14   See www.gurupolitico.com/.../el-pez-por-su-boca-muere-las-150-**frases.** Several newspaper columnists and reporters that I know chidingly describe politics as the country's most lucrative business and corruption as an inherent way of making it profitable.

becoming increasingly isolated from the electorate. This was particularly true in Mexico where the constitution granted an overwhelming amount of power to presidents and governors. Until reforms triggered by the student uprising in 1968, Mexican law, written and unwritten, prohibited criticism of the president or his policies. Front page articles concerning them were written by the chief executive's public information staff and published without change in the country's leading newspapers.

For over seventy years (1928-2000) the PRI not only controlled the executive but the legislatures and the courts as well. Although Vicente Fox campaigned as a representative of democratic change in 2000, neither he nor the party he represented, the pro-Catholic and conservative PAN, did little to alter this political structure, although Fox had to deal with active minority opposition in the Legislature and the Senate.

He and his administration floundered when they attempted to push a change that would have added sales tax on medicines and food without their having first forged agreements with other political players, including governors, the press, and the legislature. As Fox's popularity faded, he isolated himself from the electorate and devoted much of the remainder of his six-year term to sophisms based on his experience as president of Coca-Cola de Mexico ("Tell the people how good your product is often enough and they'll buy it.")

His successor, Felipe Calderón, proved to be no better a negotiator when he tried to manipulate a change in Mexico's constitution that would open Pemex to transnational investors. Legislators reacted to public pressure and stalled the reform but did not legislate against the granting of concessions to foreign corporations by administrative means.

In the early 1990s when the United States and Mexico negotiated the NAFTA, administration officials and legislators focused more on selling what actually were drastic changes to economic policy than on revealing or explaining how the agreement would affect workers, small business owners, and farmers. The result for Mexico proved disastrous, facilitating the wealth being accumulated by a few entrepreneurs and impoverishing millions of formerly self-sufficient, small producers. Mexico's economy, based on the export of raw materials, primarily oil but also lumber, pork, cotton, gold and silver, and other products and dominated by transnational enterprises, made the country increasingly dependent on foreign investment and trade instead of strengthening domestic production and employment.

In order to modernize and to compete internationally, Mexico borrowed heavily from the World Bank and the United States. Repayment of these loans, made in dollars, devoured nearly 60 percent of the country's gross national product and became even more onerous and more difficult to pay as the peso's value vis-à-vis the dollar declined. (This proved true not only for the country but for individual corporations and businesses that had borrowed in dollars but whose revenues were in pesos.) Like a wage earner with declining financial power who borrowed to meet expenses and who a short while later, unable to meet both daily obligations and repay the loan, borrowed again using a house or other possessions as collateral, Mexico burrowed more deeply into debt and into greater dependence on the lending institutions and raw material purchasers.

What can a wage earner who's losing everything do? Commit suicide? Become an itinerant dependent upon charity? Or enter into collusion with the only ones on the scene who have accessible financing, even though their activities are illegal?

The drug organizations operating in Mexico exemplified what "free enterprise" is about: developing and marketing a product that satisfies willing customers. But lacking legitimacy and confronting militarized campaigns against producing and distributing their product, they created underground networks that not only included the banking, construction, and tourist industries but *debajo el agua* government cooperation and support. As this clandestine process became more involved, Mexican federal and state governments found themselves on both sides of the equation: Surreptitiously, they (or important segments of their hierarchy) were involved financially—i.e. supporting—

15

with the enemy they were supposedly fighting. A no win situation.

The U.S. government faced a similar equation: they promoted and militarily equipped the war on drugs, theoretically, to prohibit its citizenry from using the multi-billion dollar products being imported without altering the market for them. That increased the risk for suppliers, who responded by militarizing their own enterprises. The result: Over 60,000 violent deaths, thousands of disappearances, broken homes, bankrupt businesses, and threats to national security. Another no win situation. A very expensive one!

Simultaneously, The United States militarized its campaign against undocumented workers without attempting to deal with the demand for the inexpensive labor they provided, i.e. attacking the symptoms instead of investigating the disease. As a consequence, many potential workers faced with being "illegal" as emigrant laborers chose the also-illegality of working for drug corporations.

The social repercussions of the War on Drugs terrorized huge segments of Mexico's population and bred distrust of the governments of both countries. Since those engaged in the drug trade were better organized—and in many cases better armed—than those trying to stop them, their successes spawned a multitude of associated criminal activities that made a no-man's-land of the U.S.-Mexico border and many areas in Mexico.

While political leaders of both countries could overlook or ignore the fallout from militarized actions, the so-called "collateral damage," citizens directly affected by deprivations and repressions couldn't. Nor could they overlook how government-conceded alterations to the physical environment affected their lifestyles and abilities to earn a living. Protest movements gained force and magnitude throughout the first decade of the twenty-first century, putting the government in the position of having to repress its own citizenry in order to satisfy its financial obligations to lending institutions and the transnational corporations that had gained enormous power since the passage of the Free Trade Agreement.

Covering up or repressing popular responses to landmines like the war on drugs, immigration, political corruption, and the devastation of the ecology not only created a climate of distrust and frustration but separated the leadership of the two countries from the desires and preoccupations of huge segments of their populations. "A government that doesn't give a damn about its people creates people who don't give a damn about their government." That Truman-era cliché defined the tinderbox that Mexico had become by 2010.

Drug commerce and migration-linked violence no longer could be defined as separate issues that could be resolved by legislation. Both were interwoven into the economies of the two nations; any steps to alter them affected agriculture, banking, construction, transportation, manufacturing, and the daily lives and livelihoods of millions of people. Unenforceable laws bred corruption in both government and the private sector, creating near-feudal separation between the wealthy and a serf-like majority sinking more deeply and desperately into poverty.

Protests threatened the status quo on which the economies were based, necessitating repression that in turn triggered propaganda campaigns to obscure what actually was happening. The more removed from the populace that those making governmental decisions became, the greater the fantasyland in which they and those struggling to live from one day to the next found themselves immersed.

The landmines were set to go off. One misstep and any one of them could explode.

SECTION I - MIGRATION

1

Superficial definitions and superficial solutions have failed to alter the ongoing complexity of emigration from Mexico, border barriers, unregulated payments, electronic remittances, and ICE raids. Everything that has happened with and to this workforce during the past century has impacted the economic, social, and political lives of millions of people who, although disconnected from the actual migration process, nevertheless benefitted from or suffered because of it.

Lawmakers in both countries, torn between simultaneously dealing with employers' and workers' needs and responding to constituents' perceptions and prejudices, spent billions of dollars in attempts to deter the immigrant flow and make entry more hazardous without substantially changing employer or jobseeker patterns. An estimated 580,000 Mexican citizens successfully emigrated each year during the first decade of the twenty-first century; few of them returned permanently to their communities of origin.

Law enforcement in the United States, focused on apprehending individuals, ignored employer inducements and hiring procedures, perpetuating a cycle of illegal entry, and substandard pay and unregulated living and working conditions. Seldom mentioned in bilateral discussions were how deeply involved each government had been in establishing a system that provided over twenty million workers from Latin America for U.S. industry and agriculture, nor how deeply ingrained the dependencies of both countries on this labor flow had become.

2

The traditional subsistence agriculture of western and central Mexico and the increasing demand for temporary labor in the United States combined to form a dynamic that expanded rapidly after World War II. An unplanned consequence of the seemingly endless labor supply available to U.S. agriculture was the expansion of labor-intensive food production during a time of rapid technological advancement in other fields. As long as low-wage workers were available, employers chose to rely on them rather than turn to machine-driven systems of planting, thinning, weeding, harvesting, and packing.

The dwindling number of family farms and investment in agriculture by entrepreneurs and corporations helped create a complex system of supply and demand, much of it unwritten and quasi-legal. The workers highly desired by both agriculture and the expanding food production and construction and service industries were rejected by the U.S. legal system without an examination of their recruitment, open and clandestine, by those who hired them.

Throughout the latter half of the twentieth century, Mexican families considered becoming an *indocumentado*, a viable way earn an income. (In many parts of Mexico, it became the expected way to do so.) Mexican president Gustavo Díaz Ordaz tried to negotiate guest worker agreements with the U.S. government throughout his six-year term from 1964 to 1970, but American growers and industry owners were lukewarm to the idea of a rejuvenated *bracero* program that would require them to provide government-inspected housing and detailed payroll documents.[15] They preferred to hire *indocumentados*, pay them as little as possible, and not have to deal with bureaucratic red tape.

In *Merchants of Labor*, Ernesto Galarza affirmed that besides proving war-strapped U.S. agriculture with a small legal workforce, the *bracero* program greatly stimulated

---

15   *Bracero* derives from the Spanish noun *brazo—arm: a bracero* is a "strong arm."

undocumented immigration.[16] Large agricultural corporations and packing and processing plants recruited openly in border areas and in areas where their Mexican contacts had working connections. U.S. employers quickly learned that they did not have to pay workers recruited from Mexico—legal and undocumented—medical, retirement, or union costs, and they were much less likely to seek other work than local residents were.

Mexican immigrants began following seasonal agricultural work from the border to as far north as Washington in the western United States and Michigan in the Midwest. Knowledge that work was available spread quickly through northern and central Mexico, and more and more emigrants crossed. Diaz Ordaz's successor, Luis Echeverría, pushed for even more beneficial labor terms, including allowing guest workers to remain in the United States and not be required to return to Mexico. But in October 1974, he abruptly reversed course. He told U.S. president Gerald Ford that Mexico no longer wanted any kind of guest worker accord.

Echeverría was lying. Or at best concealing what his economic advisors were telling him. The money being sent to Mexico by these emigrants, legal and undocumented, not only had relieved a severe unemployment problem but enabled Mexico's federal government to reduce by millions of pesos funds they otherwise would have dedicated to social needs. The emigrants cost the government nothing; they used none of their country's material resources, yet they contributed an estimated 30 percent of their earnings to families living in Mexico.[17]

Jorge A. Bustamante, the former president of the Colegio de Frontera Norte in Tijuana, insisted that the United States wanted to guarantee cheap labor for agribusiness and industry in order to continue to dominate

---

16 Ernesto Galarza, *Merchants of Labor: the Mexican Bracero Story* (1964).

17 The National University of Mexico (UNAM) reported in 1996 that immigrants comprised 3.6 percent of the U. S. labor force and that over 15 percent of Mexico's economically active population were immigrants working in the United States. Cited in *Viva,* April 15, 1996.

world markets. The persecution and maltreatment of *indocumentados* guaranteed that as criminals they had no rights to seek better wages, to strike, or to improve conditions where they worked or lived.[18] In *Dying To Live*, Joseph Nevins points out that U.S. foreign policy since the early nineteenth century has been based on "Manifest Destiny" that "embodied ideas of Anglo-Saxon superiority and racism, combined with an expansionist ideology that embraced a view of the United States as a beneficent power with a right and duty to conquer other hands and peoples."[19]

"'Workin' here is one thing, livin' here's another,'" a Riverside County, California journalist quoted orange growers in a conversation I had with him. "'We don' want 'em [Mexican immigrants] dirtying up our neighborhoods!'"

That attitude had pervaded United States-Mexico negotiations since the annexation of Texas in 1846. To the Anglo-Saxon mentality, Mexico was not European, although the descendants of Europeans lived there; it was primarily *indigena*, i.e. less civilized, cruder and inferior to the Europeanized United States. Although Mexican intellectuals and diplomats were treated with respect, they typically were considered "exceptions" not representatives of a political or cultural entity equal to the United States or the countries of Western Europe.[20]

Mexico's political structure derives from the centralized authority exercised by the *conquistadores* (and before them the Aztec and Mayan autocracies in central and southern Mexico). The current "democratic" governing process is highly centralized and emphasizes executive authority, much like the centuries-old *patrón* system when the owners of huge haciendas were virtual dictators who passed out favors and punishments as they saw fit. Control of governmental functions stayed in the hands of

---

18   Jorge A. Bustamante, "Migraciòn internacional y derechos humanos," 2002.
19   Joseph Nevins, *Dying To Live* (2008).
20   As late as 1999, a California college graduate, a small boat designer, and a musician interrupted a conversation about my living in Mexico with the statement, "In no way can I picture there being Mexican doctors and engineers and university professors. I can only picture illiterate field workers."

100 or so wealthy and influential families despite the chaos of the revolutionary years during the early part of the twentieth century. Clear demarcations between the haves and the have-nots remained evident.

For more than a century a growing percentage of have-nots sought work in the United States. Many of them returned to Mexico with bitter remembrances of their experiences, but millions made a transition to life north of the border, or through the money they acquired, they established homes and livelihoods in their places of origin. Their successes stimulated greater migration until in many parts of Mexico adolescent men assumed that they would migrate and share part of their earnings with family members who remained behind.[21]

Because propaganda in both countries focused on national rights, revenues, and patriotisms, the emigrants as people with needs, feelings, and personalities were very much on their own. U.S. employers often failed to check the legitimacy of social security cards and work permits and few offered vacation time or health benefits.[22] Until 2006, neither the border patrol nor local law enforcement focused on sanctioning employers, even those who obviously were hiring *indocumentados* and forcing them to live in what amounted to slave labor camps.

During the first year of his 2000-2006 term, Mexican president Vicente Fox commended the contributions emigrants were making to Mexico's economy and boasted that he and his *"amigou"*—newly elected U.S. President George Bush—would forge a solution to the problems of unrestricted and undocumented immigration.[23] Journalists

---

21 Not only families but entire communities in Mexico (and in Central America) became dependent upon the migration process. A young *campesino* in San Isidro Vista Hermosa, Oaxaca told me in 2007 that a few men remained behind "to take care of the land and the women" every year, and those who crossed the border to work in the Carolinas gave them a percentage of their earnings.

22 A Los Angeles restaurant owner in 1991 told me, "I know the documents they showed me are fake, and they know that I know that they're fake, but that's the way the game is played."

23 *Amigou,* Fox's ruralized pronunciation of the word "amigo," was one of many of the president's localisms that opposition journalists and legislators used to deride his lack of urbanity.

on both sides of the border cited similarities between the two presidents, both of whom were elected in 2000: pro-business, pro-globalization conservatives with strong entrepreneurial backgrounds and self-styled Marlboro man images. But the *amigou* relationship was heavily one-sided on Fox's part and a proposed summit meeting to resolve immigration issues, scheduled for mid-September 2001, fell by the wayside after the attack on the World Trade Center.

Instead, Immigration and Customs Enforcement (ICE), formed in 2003 as the investigating and prosecuting arm of the Department of Homeland Security, launched a concentrated series of workplace raids. Coordination with the Social Security administration to trace possession of social security numbers by computer led to stricter hiring procedures and permitted agents to inspect employers' financial and payroll records. Although arrests and deportations reduced the total undocumented immigrant population by less than 4 percent, it did force many who'd entered the United States without documents to reevaluate their emigration.

ICE spokespersons in Washington, D.C. insisted that border vigilance was "deeply focused" on preventing the entry of terrorists, would be terrorists, and those who support or equipped terrorist activities, but I found no evidence among the records of arrests and deportations that the Bureau of Border and Customs Protection made between 2003 and 2006 that any member of the agency had detected or arrested any terrorists. (Unless, as one of the ICE spokespersons retaliated icily, "They [the *indocumentados*] all may be terrorists.")

This fear of penetration of the borders by terrorists didn't begin with the attack on the World Trade Center. President Franklin D. Roosevelt's administration doubled the size of the Border Patrol from some 750 agents to nearly 1,500 in 1940 to detect the possible entrance of enemy agents or saboteurs. Throughout prohibition, the patrol's primary function was focused on intercepting rum runners, particularly along the United States-Canadian border, and during World War II, its agents guarded prison camps and patrolled the Atlantic and Pacific coasts.

Until the mid-1970s, most *indocumentados* maintained homes in Mexico and returned to them when they weren't actually employed. One of these workers, who later retired to northern California, told me he went back and forth from Tecate, Baja California, to Southern California at least a dozen times a year and only once was stopped by the *migra*. Even then, he laughed, the Border Patrol agent let him enter "because I was polite and I hadn't been drinking."

During World War II, the U.S. government forcibly evacuated citizens of Japanese ancestry from states along the western seaboard and interned them in prisoner of war-type compounds in Colorado and other mountain West areas. Many immigrants of Italian and German ancestry were investigated or harassed, but Mexican workers were needed; although they were treated as second-class citizens, immigration authorities let them enter the country with almost no restrictions.

Despite increased expenditures on sophisticated detection equipment and manpower, arrests and deportations actually declined during the first years of the Bush administration.[24] U.S. Department of Homeland Security statistics indicate that deportations steadily increased from slightly more than 1,150,000 in 1990 to slightly over 1,860,000 in 2000, then dipped to slightly less than 1,100,000 in 2003 and slightly less than 1,200,000 in 2005. Significant is the fact that voluntary departures throughout this period also decreased, a further indication that many *indocumentados* chose to stay in the United States rather than return to their homelands and risk trying to re-enter the country.

ICE's budget grew 53 percent from 2003 to 2006, reaching US$3.6 billion that year. Another US$10 billion—increased to thirteen billion for 2008—was dedicated to border control and internal enforcement of immigration law. Rhetoric that accompanied congressional approval of these expenditures fanned anti-immigrant and anti-

---

24 Between 1986 and 2002, funding for the US Border Patrol, then part of the Immigration and Naturalization Service (INS) in the Department of Justice, increased 519 percent, from $268 million in 1986 to $1.6 billion in 2002.

Mexican feelings without diminishing industry's and agriculture's hiring of needed minimum wage (and below minimum wage) employees.[25]

Alfredo Gutiérrez, a community leader in Arizona, told *Associated Press*'s Amanda Lee Myers in January 2007 that the intensity of the raids and new restrictive employer laws in that state were causing panic among *indocumentados*, where an estimated one out of ten workers lacked proper authorization.[26] Nevertheless, most *indocumentados* were determined to stay in the United States, cognizant that even with the raids and new state legislations like those in Arizona, they were better off than they would be in Mexico, where escalating crime, inflation, and rural and urban poverty made supporting oneself and one's family impossible.

A great many immigrants, born and reared in deprivation, accepted hardships as a condition of life. The hardships they encountered in the United States were different from those they had faced in Mexico, but were not so drastically different that they felt they couldn't work their way through them. As several *indocumentados* told Myers, and as many have told me, in the United States there is a hope—a possibility—that one can better himself or herself and that one's children will grow up with more opportunities than they would have in Mexico.

Throughout the 1990s and the first decade of the twenty-first century, the Mexican-born population in the United States increased by an estimated 580,000 per year —a statistic that remained relatively constant despite apprehensions, sophisticated detection equipment, and workshop raids.[27] Despite criticisms that they didn't assimilate to the "American dream" nearly one-fourth of the Mexican-born residents living in the United States in 2009 had become naturalized citizens, a figure that would

---

25 Ibid.

26 *Associated Press*, September 18, 2007. The figure nationally is one out of twenty—5 percent—according to a 2004 Urban Institute report.

27 Conapo reported in 2009 that 1.4 million citizenship applications were filed by Mexican immigrants in 2007 alone, although only 122,000 became U.S. citizens during that same year.

have been considerably higher if the hundreds of thousands who sought legal status had been allowed to apply.

According to Mexico's National Council of Population (Conapo), the greatest numbers of Latin American emigrants—70 percent—lived and worked in California, Arizona, Texas, and Illinois. An equal percentage were between fifteen and forty-four years of age. The majority— over half of the immigrants—had completed less than twelve years of formal education. Contrary to popular concepts, only an estimated 4 percent were employed in agriculture, slightly over half of whom were undocumented, principally teenaged and first-time immigrants. The majority of those working in the United States—an estimated 40 percent—were employed in manufacturing, and the rest in what Conapo loosely defined as "services," i.e. restaurants, hotels, transportation, warehouses, as gardeners and domestics, etc.

In contrast with the ebb and flow of *bracero* farm labor, where workers returned to Mexico during the off seasons, the majority of *indocumentados* entering the United States after 1990 found jobs that offered year-round employment to both men and women and enabled them to establish families and send their children to U.S. schools. Conversations that Rosa Arcelia Castellanos conducted over a five-year period with families of emigrants from the state of Veracruz led her to believe that a large percentage of emigrants from that state would have continued migrating seasonally had the *"migra"* not made crossing the border so difficult.[28]

Farm labor contractors in Florida, Georgia, and the Carolinas complained that a constant need for "new blood" existed for citrus and vegetable harvests, due in large part to the numbers of former laborers who had moved into construction and other year-round work. But both the Republican and Democratic administrations focused solely on the "immigrant" aspect of this complex worker-employment-merchandising situation and tightened

---

28 Rosa Arcelia Castellanos, e-mail correspondence with the author. *Migra*—short for *migración* is a term popularly applied to migration police (i.e. the Border Patrol).

restrictions against unauthorized entry instead of formulating a policy that would have provided for both labor and worker exigencies.

Instead of returning seasonally to their home communities, immigrant Mexican workers moved into towns and cities along the Eastern seaboard that previously had had little contact with Mexicans or Mexico, often congregating in older neighborhoods and establishing take-out food stands, Mexican bakeries, repair shops, and stores that catered to the immigrant population. Many of these newly forming communities maintained direct ties with their communities of origin in Mexico and helped relatives from them to immigrate. By 2006, 4 percent of the U.S. population of 296 million was considered to lack proper documentation, an estimated 60 percent of whom—seven million—were Mexican-born, and approximately 15 percent were children.[29]

Conflicts between these newcomers and older, established residents often were more vitriolic in the East and the South than in the central part of the United States, where immigration had proceeded more slowly and agriculture and farm-supplied industry was more closely tied to local production. Residents of several states—Iowa, Nebraska, Missouri, and Arkansas among them—angrily protested the way that ICE conducted raids on meat packing and poultry producing plants in 2004-2005. The federal officials, taken aback by the vehemence and magnitude of the protests, softened their rhetoric and released many of those they'd arbitrarily arrested, particularly those who had dependent children. Among those most vehement in these protests were a number of local mayors and sheriffs.[30]

The complaints prompted ICE to be more responsive to local authorities and to include them in the planning and carrying out of investigations, but the raids and overnight deportations continued without regard to social or

29   Pew Hispanic Center, "Modes of Entry for the Unauthorized
      Migrant Population," 2006.
30   *Arkansas Democrat-Gazette*, 2005. I deal with this in more detail
      in *Why Immigrants Come to America: Braceros, Indocumentados
      and the Migra* (2008).

economic ruptures for either the immigrant or the non-immigrant communities. ICE's insistence on "complying with the mission delegated to us by Congress," in the words of one ICE spokeswoman who refused to give a name, defined their involvement essentially as one of criminal pursuit. Given the authority to deport *indocumentados* without trial or appeal, they did so despite community complaints or complaints from human rights agencies that detailed abuses of authority, mistaken identity in deportations, and use of excessive force.

3

Seldom throughout the history of this massive movement of millions of people between the two countries did either the U.S. or the Mexican government show more than cursory concern for the social and culture changes the law enforcement actions were creating. The migration of so many heads of household ruptured the traditional structure of Mexican family life, leaving to women many responsibilities that previously had been denied them but also making many of them dependent upon money being remitted to them from absent partners. Throughout western and southern Mexico, children grew up assuming that they would leave their homes and head for the United States when they were in their teens.

Teenagers who migrated generally were considered functioning adults while they were working but immature and irresponsible adolescents when they were drinking or buying flashy clothes or joyriding in cars or on motorbikes.[31] No longer did they choose partners and marry within their communities when they were in their late teens; in their absence, many young single women also left their communities to seek work in cities or to cross into the United States. Average family size in rural communities declined to less than half of what it had been fifty years earlier.

---

31 Gloria Zafra and Magdalena López-Rocha, *Impacto de la migración en el papel de las mujeres en el ámbito publico* (2005).

Many who did return to their places of origin, Gloria Zafra and Magdalena López-Rocha assert, brought *"cholo"* customs with them—independence, drug use, slang—creating imitators among younger residents. Traditional patterns of respect and obedience to parents, teachers, and priests that had typified Mexican community life for generations were no longer taken for granted in many rural homes and workplaces. These young people no longer fit into their communities of origin, nor did they fit into urban Mexican life or into the immigrant societies in the United States. Their lack of belonging created what Mexico City priest René Jiménez described as a "a rootless agglomeration of young people who've lost faith in government, society, and religion."[32]

During the 1980s and early 1990s, Mexico's pro-globalization presidents, encouraged (or directed) by the World Bank, were determined to reduce the number of land-owning *campesinos* from twenty-five million, nearly one-fourth of the country's population, to a mere three million. The government withdrew agricultural subsidies, particularly of fertilizers and seeds, and did away with government-operated rural loan banks. Between 1990 and 2005, nearly half of the nation's rural landholders lost their lands, their incomes, and their ability to feed and clothe themselves and their families. The majority of them migrated, either to Mexican cities or the United States. Unlike previous emigrants, they had nothing in their home communities to go back to. One Oaxacan woman told me that "Only those who fail (to find and keep jobs in the United States) return."

Nearly 80 percent of Mexico's population now live in urban areas, disconnected from traditional communal roots, and an estimated 40 percent of the towns and villages in rural Mexico have experienced a population loss as high as 70 percent. Urbanization, combined with ongoing migration, resulted in a dramatic increase in the number of single-parent families, homeless, and runaway children and created an ambience that allowed petty crime and gang membership to proliferate.

---

32 Conversations with Father Rene Jiménez in Mexico City in 2007.

29

Gang membership and crime also proliferated among immigrant communities in the United States.

"I grew up living in constant apprehension," a Southern California woman, Mayra Zárate, told me.

My parents were on edge every time I or one of my sisters left the house. My father was a legal immigrant, but my mother wasn't, and the *migra* (Border Patrol) deported us even if we were U.S. citizens, so we were afraid to go to the police with any kind of complaint. We tried to stay within our community—Mexican—because there was some security there. But it became more and more dangerous. Finally when I was in high school, we were able to move.

Although employment was often easier to obtain in cities, they became "dumping grounds" for successive waves of immigrants who moved into what available housing they could find, displacing previous residents and triggering ethnic rivalries. Being able to move back and forth from Southern California to Mexico provided a "safety valve" for seasonal employment and economic dips for Mexican workers, but year by year, greater numbers of them established permanent residency in the United States.

Agricultural workers who followed the growing seasons from Southern California into Oregon, Washington, and Idaho settled in Southern California, Arizona, and Texas instead of returning to Mexico. As many of them sought—and found—temporary or year-round work, business and industry responded by hiring greater numbers of Spanish-speaking immigrants. The Hispanic communities themselves provided more and more sources of employment as small enterprises fulfilled community demands for services, food, appliances, and clothing.[33] Intermarriage between *indocumentados* and legal residents

---

33 Typical of entrepreneurial ingenuity were families who followed garage sales offering to clean up and cart off unsold discards and rubble after the sales closed. They then cleaned, mended, and repaired, and sold these items in makeshift, neighborhood, secondhand stores and bazaars.

was common; young, year-round residents did not want to pull their children in and out of school.

Nevertheless, many teenagers and the children of older —and often legalized—immigrants, unable to find adequate employment or angered by anti-Hispanic prejudices and attitudes, reverted to criminal activities, particularly gang-involved drug sales and drug use. Jammed into city barrios, unable to contend with the demands of schooling in a language—English—that they barely understood and often neglected by parents who were working long hours, they sought recognition—acceptance—from those most willing to recruit and *cuatear* with them.[34]

As the U.S. Border Patrol increased the number of agents and electronic surveillance devices and constructed walls across major immigration paths, the "safety valve" disintegrated. Many immigrants, particularly those from central and southern Mexico, cancelled trips to their home communities during slack times for fear of not being able to return to the United States without being apprehended. Thousands of migrants "disappeared" after they lost their employment or suffered reduced earnings. Others ended contact with those in their home communities because of drug or alcohol addiction or because they connected with new partners and started new families in the United States.

Abuses against those trying to cross the border without authorization have been well-documented although the media "slant" has differed from one country to the other. In contrast with propaganda and popular beliefs in both countries, nearly 50 percent of *indocumentados* entered the United States legally but were living in the country with paperwork that was no longer valid.[35] Although talk show

---

34 *"Cuatear,"* a word often not found in Spanish-English dictionaries, derives from the noun *cuate*, technically "twin" but in Mexican slang indicates a *compadre,* or "buddy."

35 The Pew Hispanic Center reported that 45 percent of *indocumentados* had entered the United States legally but had remained in the country after their documentation had expired. The percentage of Mexican nationals may be slightly lower since the Pew Center statistics covers all unauthorized entrants, and those from Europe, Africa, and Asia often had student or visitor visas to enter legally.

hosts and anti-immigration groups continued to accuse them of coming to the United States in order to become government dependents, legislation passed during the Clinton administration excluded *indocumentados* from all federal public welfare programs.

According to statistics published by the Urban Institute in 2004, 96 percent of male unauthorized immigrants worked full or nearly full-time. Percentages for legal immigrants and for U.S. citizens were considerably lower.[36] The U.S. Internal Revenue Service provided them with individual taxpayer identification numbers so they could file end-of-the-year income tax statements even though federal laws restricted their receiving benefits. Other functions of the U.S. federal government were not so accommodating. While ICE deported apprehended *indocumentados* within twenty-four hours, many of the 1.8 million children listed as "unauthorized" had legal rights to residency but had waited as long as seven years for the Department of State to approve their applications.[37]

In 2008 the National Network of Immigrant and Refugee Rights (NNIRR) blasted the militarization of the Mexico-U.S. border and the "misguided" politicization of fear of terrorism that generated arrests for racial profiling, encouraged illegal detentions, and prompted state and local governments to pass repressive anti-immigrant legislation.[38] The groups' investigations particularly called to account the criminalization of job seekers and punitive actions that permitted border patrol agents and other law enforcement personnel to pursue and manhandle suspected *indocumentados* without regard to constitutional restraints.

---

36 Undocumented Immigrants: Facts and Figures, Urban Institute, 2004.

37 United States Department of State "Visa Bulletin," 2006. However, the U.S. Citizen and Immigrant Services (UCSIS) reported that as of October 2007, it was processing some family-related visa checks filed as far back as 1985 and was still processing some employment-related visa applications from 2001.

38 "Over Raided, Under Siege," National Network for Immigrant and Refugee Rights, 2008.

Like many investigations that preceded and followed it, the report failed to have any noticeable effect on lawmakers' decisions. New regulations passed by federal and state governments encouraged rather than lessened criminal activities by making it necessary for would-be immigrants to hire *coyotes* equipped with smuggling vans, safe houses, and multiple guides. Criminalizing the immigrants rather than those who hired them encouraged labor bosses and employers to pay less-than-minimum-wages, to deduct for taxes and social security that they never remitted to the government and to fire workers without paying earnings due to them.

Because these workers were considered "illegals"—i.e. lawbreakers—appealing such abuses often resulted in deportation. A 2008 report indicated that more than 300,000 *indocumentados* were incarcerated "under migratory custody" in the United States. Although the average time of incarceration was thirty-eight days, many of these immigrants had been held for four and five months while their cases were being investigated.[39] Medical attention in these facilities, most of which were privately owned and under contract to the federal government, was virtually non-existent, and an Oaxacan who had been held for nearly two months in a detention center in Texas told me the food "was worse than one could pull out of garbage cans."

The racial profiling described in the NNIRR investigations was not new. Under "Operation Wetback" in the early 1950s, the United States deported over two million Mexicans (a large number of whom were U.S. citizens).[40] During the economic revival in the mid-1950s, deportations virtually ceased and did not increase substantially for nearly a decade, peaking again in the 1970s. U.S. president Jimmy Carter authorized the construction of the so-called "Tortilla Curtain" to restrict immigrants from entering the United States through El Paso, Texas. His successor Ronald Reagan, assuming that

39 Arturo Cano, *Migrantes detenidos en EA pierden libertad ... y salud, La Jornada noticias* online, April 22, 2010
40 Monica Verea, *Entre México y Estados Unidos: los indocumentados* (1982).

indocumentados were taking employment away from U.S. citizens, inaugurated "Project Jobs" to purge the country of illegal workers. Law enforcement agents swept through farms and workplaces, detaining and deporting those who did not have authorization to live and work in the United States.[41]

Finally, after years of frustrated efforts to pass some kind of authoritative legislation, the U.S. Congress enacted the Immigration and Reform Act, more popularly known as the "Simpson-Rodino Act," in November 1986. It provided that undocumented residents who had lived in the United States for a set period of time (or farm workers who had worked at least six months for several consecutive years) could legalize their status under the act's amnesty requirements. It also increased funding for the Border Control and made hiring persons who lacked legal documentation to reside in the United State a crime punishable by fines and by jail terms for repeat offenders.

The Reagan administration announced that the Simpson-Rodino Act would legalize those who deserve to be legalized and the increased border security and employer penalties would curtail the entrance of any lacked documentation, thus enabling law enforcement to deport those who did not qualify for amnesty. Punishing those who hired *indocumentados* would constrict the flow of newcomers: If there were no jobs, there no longer would be a reason to cross the border illegally to look for them. Those with papers would stay in the United States and work; those without would leave voluntarily or would be deported.[42]

Response to the amnesty provisions was slow at first, primarily because most *indocumentados* did not trust dealing with the Immigration and Naturalization Service. But as registrations picked up, so did optimism within the

---

41 Michael Greenwood and Marta Tienda, U.S. Impacts on Mexican Migration, 1998. The authors contended that *indocumentados* seldom took jobs away from U.S. workers but frequently replaced previous undocumented workers "because the two groups are good labor market substitutes."

42 Douglas S. Massey, Jorge Durand, and Nolan J. Malone, *Beyond Smoke and Mirrors* (2002). Also Stout, *Why Immigrants Come to America* (2008).

immigrant society. The prospects that three million immigrants could gain legal residency and work status stimulated at least twice that many more to emigrate in hopes that they too could obtain residency benefits. The granting of amnesty under the Simpson-Rodino Act made the United States seem like a land of opportunity to millions in Mexico. As a result, the campaign to resolve the illegal immigration problem wound up accelerating rather than deterring undocumented entry.[43]

Concurrent with this increase in immigration, U.S. labor unions' hold on the construction industry—and other industries, such as meat packing, etc.—diminished greatly. As Mexico's economy bottomed out in the mid-1980s, hundreds of thousands of laid off workers and jobseekers surged northward. The percentage of women emigrating to seek work in the United States increased dramatically. Thousands found work as domestics; thousands of others as restaurant employees, sweatshop seamstresses, and assembly line workers.

4

I've attended a number of "homecomings" of immigrants who achieved legal status in the United States. During one of them in a small town in Oaxaca, the vacationing returnee threw a community-wide party (the Pope couldn't have been treated with more respect than he was). He later confided to me that he had a good job—as a cook in a hotel restaurant in California. In quite passable English he told me, "You think I get treated this way in L.A.? Here they give me a parade, everybody wants to

---

43 Wayne A. Cornelius, "Death at the Border," *Population and Development Review* 669, 2001. Estimations of the actual number of deaths that have occurred vary. Mexican statistics usually show a higher number than estimates from the United States, but both tally the number in the thousands. According to the Arizona *Daily Star,* 237 bodies were found during 2007 in Arizona alone. Many bodies are not found and many emigrants die from the effects of their migrations in the border cities and in the United States.

shake my hand, kiss me. *Chingada!* They're even going to name a park after me!"

He acknowledged that dozens of the town's teenagers talked to him about emigrating "so they could have the things I have. So they can send lots of money to their mothers, sisters, *novias.*" He said very few of them mentioned returning to the impoverished conditions they wanted to escape.

This escape—"safety valve"—drew increased numbers with every dip in Mexico's economy, just as deportations increased in the United States with every economic recession. One of Mexico's worst crises before 2007 occurred in 1994 during the first month of Ernesto Zedillo's six-year presidential term. Years of devoting billions of pesos to brace the value of Mexico's currency on the international exchange forced the federal government to float the peso's value (after surreptitiously notifying a few select entrepreneurs who quickly transferred their assets from pesos into dollars.)

Overnight, the value of Mexico's currency plummeted, doubling and tripling the amount of pesos those with dollar debts had incurred, crippling consumer buying power, and throwing thousands out of work. The Clinton administration's response to the heightened migration triggered by this crisis was to tighten border security, but U.S industry and agro-business willingly absorbed undocumented newcomers who would work for sub-standard wages. Mexico tried to meet international debt obligations by cutting domestic spending and bolstering banking solvency by transferring billions in entrepreneurial debt to the public sector while privately acknowledging that emigrants' remittances were replacing money that otherwise could have been dedicated to social services.

Despite Zedillo's campaign promises (and those of Mexican presidents Vicente Fox and Felipe Calderón) to generate employment within Mexico, by the turn of the twenty-first century migration northward had increased to 1,000 percent of what it had been in the 1960s. The billions being spent by the U.S. government on preventing illegal entry through the four states bordering Mexico

(California, Arizona, New Mexico, and Texas) failed to substantially reduce this flow.

Before the 1990s, a majority of emigrants found it relatively easy to enter the United States. In 2006, the Pew Hispanic Center reported that 45 percent of the *indocumentados* living in the United States had entered the country legally, often with twenty-four hour passes or entry restricted to border areas. Others purchased counterfeit green cards in border cities like Tijuana and Ciudad Juarez or "I simply took the bus to Agua Prieto, walked across the border, and a car picked me up there to take me to Phoenix," an Oaxacan who crossed the border in 1994 shrugged as he described the first days of his five-year stay in the United States. After years of increased expenditures (including Congress's approval for construction of a 700-mile wall that would cost U.S. taxpayers $2.2 billion dollars) the rate of deportations increased only slightly while the *indocumentado* population in the United States continued to rise.

However, the harsh border control measures forced many emigrants to attempt crossing isolated desert and mountain areas, resulting in a surge of deaths from heat, dehydration, and exhaustion.[44] One missed connection, one wrong turn, one accident could be fatal to those making the five- to seven-day trip from the Mexican side of the boundary to a pick up point or safe house in the United States. A would be emigrant named Eberht told me his *coyote* abandoned him and his group of six or seven somewhere on the Arizona desert.

"We were milling around, not knowing what to do, when the Border Patrol swooped in. We were glad to see them even though they dumped us right back into Mexico."[45]

Others were not so fortunate. In *Dying To Live*, Joseph Nevins describes the discovery of seven mummified bodies "so severely decomposed that the eyes were destroyed" in 120 degree heat on the desert in California's Imperial

---

44 Cornelius, Wayne A., "Death at the Border: Efficacy and Unintended Consequences of U.S. Immigration Control Policy, *Population and Development Review* 669, 2001.

45 That was his only attempt to enter the United States; unlike many, he returned to Oaxaca and did not make another attempt.

County in 1998. Apparently, the group of immigrants to which they belonged had run out of water some time before —a fatal consequence on the desert.[46] Survivors of a group who arrived safely in Phoenix in 2005 mourned three of the original fourteen left behind because one of them had broken her foot in a fall and couldn't continue. One of the survivor's parents told me that leaving the three, whose bodies were discovered weeks later, so traumatized her daughter that she no longer could remain in the United States.

"I had to pay a relative to bring her back to Mexico so she could get some kind of care," the mother remembered.

Until the late 1990s, most undocumented immigrants attempted border crossings on their own or paid self-employed *polleros* [poultry dealers] to help them. "They [the *polleros*] are people from here," Joaquín Martínez, secretary to the sectional president of Puerto Palomas de Villa on the Chihuahua-New Mexico border, explained, "but they don't do anything bad to anyone, they dedicate themselves to their business and that's it."[47] Residents of the area added that the *polleros's* earnings benefited the economy of poverty-stricken regions just as the money brought in and spent by drug exporters did.

Stricter detection measures forced many would-be immigrants to rely on criminal bands that charged exorbitant fees and often held the emigrants hostage for weeks and even months in intolerable living conditions while they extracted additional money from the hostages' relatives. These bands had contacts on both sides of the frontier and knew how the Mexican police and the U.S. Border Patrol operated. Gradually, the principal criminal organizations gobbled up smaller local operatives. ("Join us or join those in the cemetery," was the usual ultimatum.)

The bigger organizations operated throughout the country, particularly in urban areas that were transportation and shipping centers, and along Mexico's southern border. Militarized bands of *Zetas* boarded freight trains and corralled Central Americans journeying north, raping the women and holding the emigrants in prison-like

46   Joseph Nevins, *Dying To Live,* (2008).
47   *Noticias, Voz e Imagen de Oaxaca,* June 12, 2007.

jungle compounds until relatives paid from US$1,500 to US$5,000 for their release. They routinely butchered those whose contacts failed to pay the ransoms. Tens of thousands of Guatemalans, Salvadorans, and Hondurans who attempted to cross through Mexico to the United States disappeared during the first decade of the twenty-first century.

The *Zetas* distributed money to local law enforcement personnel and businessmen who cooperated with their shakedowns. Like many criminal bands operating on Mexico's northern border, they preyed on both immigrants and *coyotes* but were not directly involved in transporting people from one country to another.[48] Also, like the bands in the north, they paid regular quotas to the large drug exporting organizations for letting them operate under their aegis.

Mexican human rights activists maintained that U.S. authorities criminalized coyotes instead of investigating industry and agro-business dependence upon *indocumentados* and their willingness to hire them despite their supposed illegality. U.S. newspapers and television news headlined fatal crashes by vehicles carrying immigrants and suffocation in sealed cargo carriers, while the Mexican media bannered deaths on the desert, slayings of unarmed emigrants by Border Control officers, and the treatment of migrants in U.S. detention centers. Which was worse? Which was more inhumane? The immigrants wouldn't have crossed the border if work wasn't available, but policymakers overlooked the greater issues—cheap labor for U.S. employers and poverty in Mexico—to focus on unauthorized entry—i.e. the symptoms, not the cause.

The crackdown on unauthorized entry—armed Border Patrol, helicopters, infra-red detection devices, etc.—and workshop and neighborhood raids by ICE increased the power and territory of the drug organizations. They recruited young deportees, particularly those acquainted with U.S. geography, customs, and language. As entering the United States became more difficult among Mexican junior high school and high school students and dropouts, the cliché "My only choice to earn a living is crime or

48 *Proceso*, Sep. 6, 2009

emigration!" saw the "emigration" alternative becoming the less feasible.

5

By 2006, twenty-seven million residents of Mexican origin, including an estimated 6.6 million *indocumentados,* lived in the United States.[49] They sent over US$24 billion in remittances to relatives in Mexico in 2007 alone, 98 percent of which was used for daily living expenses (including house and equipment repairs, consumer items, and education), and only 2 percent for infrastructure or employment-generating small businesses.[50]

The US$24 billion, which began to decline late that year as the construction industry in the United States suffered a lengthy downturn, plummeted nearly 20 percent after the financial collapse. Nevertheless, the amount of remittances being sent exceeded the amount of foreign business and industry investment in Mexico and nearly equaled what was garnered by the petroleum industry, thus officially becoming the country's second largest source of income.[51] (Money brought into the country illicitly from drug exportations outstripped both remittances and Pemex earnings, but until 2009 only was recognized by non-governmental sources such as *Forbes* magazine.)

The decrease in remittances created a domino effect. Having less money, those in Mexico dependent upon remittances purchased less. School attendance declined as children dropped out in order to work, usually in low-paying, informal section jobs. Returning emigrants exacerbated an already high unemployment rate.

---

49 Urban Institute, 2006. An estimated 12-15 percent of Mexico's labor force works in the United States, and an estimated one out of seven working in Mexico migrated at least temporarily to employment in the United States.

50 Deputy Edmundo Ramírez-Martínez in a report to the House of Deputies, January 2007. In August 2007, Banco de Mexico reported that over 33.1 million individual transferences were recorded during the first six months of that year, an average of US$348 per remittance. (*El Universal,* August 24, 2007.)

51 According to Banco de Mexico statistics, remittances totaled more than income from oil exports in 2008.

Struggling retail, construction, and service industries laid off workers or closed. By September 2009, sources in Michoacán and Oaxaca were reporting a noticeable increase in "reverse remittances"—money being sent from Mexico to help support family members who'd lost their jobs in the United States.

Although unemployment figures reported by the Mexican government hovered near or below 5 percent during the decade preceding the economic collapse, actual unemployment was much greater since the statistics included only unemployed jobseekers, not adults without work. Employment in the informal section reached nearly 50 percent of domestic income by 2007, a constant aggravation to state and federal governments, because very few in the informal section paid sales or income taxes. The Mexican Electricians Union reported that 56 percent of salaried Mexican workers received less than twice the minimum wage (i.e. US$4 a day) "continuing the option of many to leave the country in search for a better opportunity."[52]

While the exodus of workers provided Mexico with a consistent flow of income, it did not compensate for the enormous waste of manpower that made its economy increasingly dependent upon the United States. Those leaving did not contribute to internal development, just as the flow of oil northward did not build up infrastructure, which could have made the country more self-sufficient. According to the United Nations Development Program in 2007, Mexico ranked behind Argentina, Chile, Uruguay, Costa Rica, and Cuba in the index of human development. While those countries were fortifying internal long-term growth potential, which included employment and production for internal consumption, Mexico was losing its capacity to do the same.[53]

Not only did the loss of manpower decrease contributions to Mexico's social security system, it

---

52 "National Project for the Defense of Salary and Employment," Center for Labor Action and Assessment (Cilas), Mexican Electricians Union (SME), 2007.

53 United Nations Development Program, Third Report of the Human Development Index, June 2007.

cushioned the U.S. social security fund by providing an estimated 10-15 percent of its annual intake—money that most of those contributing could not access, because as *indocumentados*, they were prohibited from applying for benefits of any kind.[54]

This loss of productive personnel created "a community that lives on remittances, but with the loss of productive people, the regions lose the capacity to grow in the long term," concluded the U.N.'s Felipe Luis López-Calva.[55]

For many immigrants, the better opportunity they were seeking led to bitter experiences, particularly in agricultural regions where farm labor contractors hired thousands of temporary workers. As the number of individually owned and operated farms in the United States gave way to investment agriculture—"agro-business"— those responsible for production depended more and more on farm labor contractors who were usually (but not always) U.S. citizens of Mexican birth or ancestry, who had connections with *coyote* combines or who had contacts in specific regions of Mexico that could provide workers.

Many of these contractors were capable ex-field hands who'd proved they could get the needed work done for their employers. *Indocumentados* who had just arrived in the United States frequently preferred to work for someone who spoke their language and understood their culture rather than for a gringo they couldn't relate to or understand. The contractors often paid the smuggling fees and deducted the money from the laborers wages.

Labor contractors made good money—as much as $300,000 a year by the early 1990s. Many of them not only hired the workers and arranged for their transportation and housing but handled administrative details including payroll, social security, and income tax deductions as well. Some of them pocketed part or all of this money since they could fire anyone who complained and neither the federal government nor the firms that hired the labor contractors

---

54 These contributions to the U.S. social security system by Mexican workers in the United States totaled more than $7 billion dollars a year.

55 United Nations Development Program, Third Report of the Human Development index, June 2007.

investigated how much they paid out or took in. The *indocumentados*, after all, were working illegally, which technically meant both the labor contractors and the agro-business firms were transacting illegal business by employing them.[56]

Few of the labor contractors bothered with detailed accountings; some of those who did presented misleading —or totally fictitious—expenditure and income figures. It was not uncommon for a contractor to fulfill needs for fifty or so workers with half or two-thirds that number, forcing those hired to work overtime hours while the contractor pocketed the money due to the ghost workers he listed on pay sheets that he showed his employers.

Several labor contractors that I interviewed in the early 1990s told me that they always tried to hire new immigrants, not those returning from the previous year. These new arrivals understood less about the system, usually spoke no English (and often, if they were *indigenas,* relatively little Spanish) and were desperate for money. They did not complain about long working hours, deductions from their wages, or woeful living conditions.

Other farm labor contractors operated out of their houses or their vans and imported *compañeros* from towns in Mexico where they had lived. Not only were these workers "friends of the family" who confided in the contractor, they and their families were dependent upon him for everything from food to transportation to work hours.

The need for immigrant labor was obvious to employers who hired them, whether or not the U.S. government was willing or able to admit that fact. Not only were 96 percent of male *indocumentados* employed, but an estimated 94 percent of them had jobs waiting for them before they left their communities of origin. This employment percentage

---

56 Robert Joe Stout, *Why Immigrants Come to America,* 2008. A group of Oaxacans working in the garlic fields outside of Gilroy, east of San Jose, California, in 1991 were defrauded by a contractor named "Juan" who'd given the farm owner a fictitious last name. A few weeks later, another contractor, this one named "Miguel," absconded with another two weeks of wages, leaving the immigrants penniless after more than a month of hard labor.

dropped off after the 2007-2008 economic collapse, but an anticipated massive return of immigrants to Mexico did not occur.[57]

However, thanks to NAFTA, a number of U.S. growers moved their operations to Mexico to take advantage of legal inexpensive labor and less governmental involvement in reporting procedures and the use of pesticides. During a press conference, California Senator Dianne Feinstein presented maps that pinpointed 50,000 acres of agricultural land south of the border that was being farmed by U.S. concerns.[58]

The Mexican government's refusal to utilize its petroleum resources to develop infrastructure and industry and to depend upon export aggravated unemployment and stimulated emigration. The Bush and Obama governments responded by increasing their financing of anti-immigration efforts at the same time that U.S. and transnational businesses and entrepreneurs were exploiting Mexican industry, driving many small producers and retail outlets out of business, further aggravating unemployment, and stimulating the very immigration they were trying to contain.

Not only Mexico's petroleum but 85.5 percent of its non-petroleum exports went north, triggering a massive

---

57 Seldom mentioned in the reports or included in the statistics about migration presented by either country are workers who entered the United States legally. A provision of the North American Free Trade Agreement (NAFTA) passed in 1994 authorized dual nationality, which many Mexican and American entrepreneurs (and many of us who are not entrepreneurs) obtained. In addition, many technicians, doctors, professors, and other professionals worked legally in the United States.

58 Julia Preston, "Short on Labor, Farmers in U.S. Shift to Mexico, *New York Times,* September 5, 2007. A grower told correspondent Preston that he moved his operations to Guanajuato because of frustrations with "fighting the fight on the immigration issue." Instead of paying wages of US$9 an hour, the prevailing rate in California, he hired workers for US$9 a day, which more than compensated for higher shipping and transportation costs incurred in his operations south of the border. Feinstein supported a measure in the immigration bill that Congress failed to pass during Bush's presidency that would have granted legal status to migrant agricultural workers.

collapse when U.S. industry cut back on purchases during the 2007-2009 financial crises.[59] At the same time, Mexico's largest oil field, Cantarell, began to play out, reducing the amount of crude oil available for export and limiting the government's ability to stimulate the economy. The only activity not severely affected by falling finances was the drug trade.

Residents in southern Mexico that I interviewed told me that a family needed to have permanent U.S. residents remitting money in order to survive. Many who left their home communities in Mexico intending to return after a few years remained on "the other side," because relatives in Mexico depended on the money they were sending or because they'd grown accustomed to their lives in the United States and felt alienated from their places of origin. As poverty among rural residents increased and more *campesinos* and *ejidarios* lost their land, a greater number of those who emigrated felt they had nothing to keep them in Mexico and left the country intending to settle permanently in the United States.

6

The emigration process that developed over the latter half of the twentieth century traditionally began with one family member—usually the male parent—leaving first, finding work, and sending as much money as he could to his wife and/or other family members in Mexico. As the cost of maintaining a split household, estrangement, and the problems of single parenthood increased, the emigrant would bring first his wife, then their children to live with him in the United States. Through contacts in their new environment, they would notify brothers, nephews, uncles, nieces, and hometown friends of job opportunities.

Although there were difficulties—prejudice, fear of law enforcement, layoffs, and petty crime—the children of these immigrants attended school, some dropping out because of language difficulties, others becoming effectively bilingual, playing on athletic teams and in school bands and

---

59 *El Universal,* August 24, 2007.

orchestras and competing for grades and honors. As job opportunities opened in areas that previously had had few Mexican residents, the process repeated itself with those who found work encouraging others to join them and employers taking advantage of new sources of labor to expand or to fill vacancies that they couldn't fill with local residents.

Frequently, these immigrant communities sifted into older and often sub-standard housing and made do without social benefits or community services. Often they lacked police protection. They faced similar conditions— including homophobia based on racial physical characteristics—that African-Americans had encountered when they migrated from the former slave states earlier in the twentieth century. They also lived under a sword of Damocles for being in the country illegally. But in contrast with the African-American population, they were linked socially and as families with their countries of origin. Many felt divided loyalties, and even those who felt victimized by their circumstances realized (or learned) how intertwined the economics and the politics of their two countries had become.[60]

Most Mexican-born workers in the United States did not belong to labor organizations or politically oriented NGOs. Communities developed their own internal services —everything from auto repairs to food preparation to English classes—and maintained inter-dependent and often complicated ties with communities in Mexico. The value of each contributor, each worker, was known, acknowledged; they were real people with real identities,

---

60 In the small central plaza of a little town in western Oaxaca, sipping a hot *atole* that I'd purchased at an *ambulante's* stall, I commented on the presence of a cubbyhole-sized business jammed with side-by-side computers. A woman who said she'd recently returned from four years in Texas explained that the town's *secundaria* (junior high) students had learned to use computers in school, and besides pursuing their own interests, were transmitting family and local news and gossip back and forth with their families' relatives and friends in the United States. "We learn about accidents, deportations, pregnancies, and bonus payments before we know about things that happen here at home," the woman laughed.

not merely ciphers that could be shifted from one place to another (*coyote* to job to jail) at the whim of business, agriculture, or government. They were individuals with desires, needs, and virtues; despite hardships, over twenty million of them established livelihoods and ways of coping in the United States.

Employers of the estimated twelve million undocumented workers continued to operate in a twilight area of encouraging non-authorized immigration by hiring workers without—or with false or expired—documentation. As pointed out earlier, Mexican authorities chose not to repress emigration for fear of losing the billions of dollars that the country received in remittances. They preferred to wait for the U.S. government to establish new relationships with the immigrant population in hopes that legalizing the flow of workers would keep the financial pipeline open. Now and then the Mexican government offered tepid protests about the militarization of the U.S. border and the hundreds of deaths suffered by Mexican citizens packed into locked vans and delivery trucks or trekking by foot through the southern California or Arizona deserts.

In *Dying To Live*, Nevins describes an eleven-year-old who died of hypothermia trying to cross through Arizona in July 2006. He concludes:

> Such cases expose the violence in immigration and boundary policing. It is violent in that it denies people some of their most basic rights—a right to life, to be free of inhuman or degrading treatment, a right to a standard of living adequate for the health and wellbeing of oneself and one's family ...[61]

Although Mexico's birth rate gradually decreased over the past six decades, nearly two million new jobseekers tried to wedge their way into the workforce every year. Deportees and those voluntarily returning from "the other side" swelled these ranks, as did layoffs and privatizations in Mexico. Violence on the Mexican side of the U.S.-Mexico border increased exponentially, making cities like Ciudad Juárez, Matamoros, and Reynosa virtually uninhabitable.

---

61 Joseph Nevins, *Dying To Live* (2008).

Well run and well financed criminal corporations functioned as individual nations within the country despite military operations on both sides of the frontier.

Even immigrants who'd lost their jobs in the United States, or who faced criminal charges for illegal entry, chose not to return to their communities of origin, because they had nothing to go back to except conditions that were worse than those they faced in the United States. A returned emigrant named Efrén Cruz told me in Reynosa, Tamaulipas, that "Finally one feels only anger. Anger at the corruption, the police, the struggling, people all the time insulting you, putting you down. And you want to fight back. You want to hurt someone. You don't care anymore what happens to you. You want to fight."

As increased competition among the drug corporations triggered confrontations that became bloody all-out battles, Mexican entrepreneurs moved billions of dollars from Mexican banks and assets, further debilitating the country's economy. Despite U.S. financial assistance, it could not diminish drug organization takeovers of land or the financing of its operations. It could not provide employment for tens of millions of impoverished residents of the country nor of returning emigrants forced out of the United States, a percentage of whom joined the criminal organizations, linking the drug trade to migration.

The interconnections among emigration (the "safety valve"), the drug corporations that were providing the undiminished U.S. market with its cocaine, designer drugs and marijuana, and over half a century of corruption on the part of Mexican and international businesses and politicians enmeshed the petroleum, lumber, and tourist industries and the ecological devastation they were causing in a complicated fabric that ripped with every attempted individual solution. To keep this fabric from further ripping, both industry and government repressed public protests that actually or apparently threatened to rend the situation beyond repair.

The landmines are there. It is not difficult to imagine repression and unemployment reaching the point that a police shooting or apprehension of an *indocumentado* by anti-immigrant hoodlums could ignite riots like those experienced in Washington, D. C. and Watts in the 1960s. Or retaliations against military repression and poverty in Ciudad Juárez or Reynosa sending rampaging gangs or hordes of refugees across the bridges into the United States. Or prisoners in an overcrowded privately run facility revolting, overwhelming guards, and surging through the countryside. Or drug corporations growing so powerful they dominant not only the economics between the two countries but the politics as well and ...

Boom!

Choose your scenario.

Or a place to hide.

SECTION II: THE WAR ON DRUGS

1

The rise to power of the various drug corporations drastically altered the way that Mexico had been governed since 1926. The drug mafias proved that it no longer was necessary to overthrow an existing governmental structure if an organized, disciplined power could function as a nation within the nation.[62]

The principal drug corporations established their own operating principles and rules, maintained a trained well-equipped armed force, and generated greater revenues than the political entity in which they existed. Their unpublicized payrolls included generals, governors, legislators, entrepreneurs, and law enforcement, all of whom also received regular contributions from the various exporters. By the 1970s, drug corporation participants had become so interwoven with the establishment that it became impossible to separate legitimate from illegitimate incomes and expenditures.

Until 1914, laudanum (a liquid opiate) and morphine were legally sold and distributed in the United States, heroin was prescribed as a cough medicine, and coca and cocaine were mixed with wine and cola drinks. Although most of the opium was imported from the Orient, Chinese settlers on Mexico's west coast, particularly in the state of Sinaloa, began cultivating *adormidera* during the 1870s and gradually developed an export trade.

Even after the use of opium-based products was declared illegal in the United States, the exportations from Sinaloa continued; prosecution of offenders, if they happened at all, were benign. Much of the exportation crossed into the United States through Tijuana, a dusty

62   A condensed version of this section appeared in *The Monthly Review,* January 2012.

little frontier town, until the mid-twentieth century when it shifted to include San Luis Río, Colorado, across the border from Yuma, Arizona, Nogales (also on the Arizona border), and Ojinaga, across the Rio Grande River from Presidio in Texas's isolated Big Bend country. Customs agents on both sides of the border, but particularly in Mexico, cooperated, and the flow of drugs went through virtually unimpeded.

The majority of these exporters were locals who spent the cash they acquired in the areas in which they lived and operated. They hired local residents for construction, transportation, ranching, and other sidelines in which they invested their earnings. As far as most of their neighbors were concerned, they were good citizens whose business was no better or worse from that of any other.[63]

Prohibition changed this genial and basically cooperative landscape. Large amounts of liquor were harder to conceal than *adormidera* or marijuana, making it necessary for exporters to bribe—or form partnerships—with those in charge of customs. Politicians ranging in rank from local councilmen to state governors became involved, forcing the local exporters either to join them or evade them, as well as evade law enforcement.

The end of prohibition wounded but did not slay the golden calf of liquor exportation. The politically connected entrepreneurs that controlled the *aduanas* (customs inspection stations) also controlled prostitution and a percentage of drug exportations. They financed the construction and operation of luxurious night clubs, gourmet restaurants, and gambling activities that attracted large numbers of U.S. residents. Both politically-affiliated and independent drug exporters invested in these enterprises as Tijuana, Ciudad Juárez, and other border cities became brightly lit tourist meccas surrounded by desolate slums packed with new arrivals, deportees, addicts, beggars, and petty criminals.

By 1948, the volume of Sinaloa *adormidera* crossing the border triggered harsh recriminations from representatives of the U.S. federal government.[64] The Mexico City newspapers, *Excélsior* and *Ultimas Noticias,* accused

---

63 Francisco Cruz, *El cártel de Juárez* (2008).

51

Sinaloa governor Pablo Macías and other state officeholders of prospering from and protecting drug producers. Sinaloa officials countered that the journalists were motivated solely by "the marketing voracity of the editors of the most immoral daily on the American continent."[65]

Mexico's attorney general answered U.S. complaints about drug contraband with tart suggestions that officials north of the border deal with the consumers who purchased the illegal substances. (This "It's your fault, not ours!" rhetoric about the drug trade persisted in both countries throughout the last half of the twentieth century and first decade of the twenty-first, much of it substituting for effective action on either government's part.) Nevertheless, Mexican federal and state law enforcement carried out raids and arrested a few farmers and *mulas* (mules, i.e. those hired to transport contraband), but did not prosecute any leading political or business figures.

Few high-ranking authorities in either the government of Mexico or the United States seemed to realize how thoroughly the production and exportation of opium derivatives and marijuana had become integrated into Sinaloa politics and society by the mid-1950s. Despite cinema and television depictions of drug runners as gun-toting, Pancho Villa-like gangsters, many well-attired, well-educated governors, bankers, and businessmen considered that the business of growing and exporting *adormidera*—opium poppy gum—was as natural (and as profitable) as growing cotton or corn. The income from drug exportations filtered through the state's economy and was attributed to "sale of agricultural products" if and when the source was questioned.

Mexican authorities did arrest and convict a number of smugglers and confiscate a few kilos of heroin, morphine, opium gum, and marijuana each year during the 1950s and 1960s in Sinaloa and in various border points,

---

64 The state of Sinaloa twines for slightly over 500 kilometers along Mexico's west coast and includes the port cities of Los Mochis and Mazatlan.

65 Referring to the Mexico City daily *Excélsior*. Luis Astorga, *El siglo de las drogas* (2005).

particularly Tijuana. However, the most publicized busts occurred in Mexico City where agents intercepted heroin shipments from France and arrested a young traveler with ten kilos of heroin in 1964, and a professor importing pure heroin from Peru in 1968.[66]

As marijuana and cocaine use increased exponentially during the 1960s in the United States, many Mexican drug exporters expanded their operations, keeping control within their families and circles of close friends. Because they needed to do something with the immense amounts of cash they were receiving, they purchased cars and condominiums and ranches. (One could have a property transaction legally notarized for a sale price of one-tenth or one-twentieth of the actual amount paid; the remaining 80 or 90 percent flowed into the local economy without its origin being traced.)

To buy or build a condominium, one had to pay construction workers and their suppliers, plus local taxes and transportation; to buy and operate a ranch, one had to purchase cattle, feed, heavy equipment, and build reservoirs and roads. Few of those receiving this cash were criminals or delinquents or had any connections with organized crime, and they spent the cash they received on everything from school tuition and church tithes to sports tickets and Disneyland vacations. Columbia University and Instituto Tecnológico de Mexico professor Edgardo Buscaglia told *Proceso* in 2009 that his research confirmed that 78 percent of the money legally circulating in Mexico originated with the drug trade.[67]

As the Sinaloa drug entrepreneurs expanded, solidifying their internal structure and involvement in the political system, they established bases in other parts of the country, particularly along the Mexico-United States border. Most of them kept control of their businesses within their families and circles of close friends, but as they moved into other areas, particularly Tamaulipas in northeastern Mexico, they clashed with exporters there who, though not as effectively organized, had greater

---

66 Ibid.
67 *La estructura financiera del narco, intocada, Proceso,* March 15, 2009.

access to delivery points across the border. They also competed for connections with the major Colombian "cartels," whose influence and political power had increased dramatically.

By the 1970s, importing plane *loads* of cocaine, transporting it to border points, and getting it into the United had become an increasingly complex affair, and the drug organizations had become intricately organized businesses that included accountants, lawyers, chemists, legislators, and entire corps of police. Clearly defined chains of command were departmentalized into individual functions, which included marketing, investment, press relations, and militarized units, most of which were led by experienced former Mexican Army and Navy officers.

As they grew they brought more elements of Mexican society into their operations, particularly for laundering their profits and for transporting drugs. Tourists and businessmen and women—well-dressed, affable, polite— crossed the border carrying false bottomed luggage that concealed cocaine. Soccer balls and balloons contained packets of powder. Brassieres that made small-breasted women seem much more amply endowed were padded with cocaine sewed into the garments. According to retired U.S. Air Force journalist James McGee, importers in El Paso brought thousands of colorful Mexican piñatas across the border—piñatas that were never retailed but ripped open and discarded after the cocaine packed inside them had been removed.[68]

Detections of drug contraband were frequent but seldom impacted the overall process. One exception: tipped off by a Baja California state police officer who'd infiltrated the brothers Arellano-Felix's Tijuana cartel in 1989, U.S. authorities decommissioned twenty-one *tons* of cocaine worth an estimated 7.1 *billion* dollars in a warehouse in Sylmar, California.[69] The Colombian exporters and their Mexican counterparts shrugged off lesser losses, even those that reached millions of dollars in potential street

---

68 Conversations with McGee in Riverside, California, 1986.
69 Michael Connelly and Eric Malnic, "Record 20 Tons of Cocaine Seized," *Los Angeles Times,* February 4, 1989.

sales. "There is more, there always is more," had become the password, both for drugs and money.

As happens with most corporations, junior operatives (executives) broke away to form smaller organizations of their own. Murders and assassinations between rival bands increased as they vied for portions of the lucrative trade. Breakaway groups unable to chisel a large enough portion for themselves branched into other criminal activities—people smuggling, counterfeiting, business shakedowns, prostitution, auto theft, and kidnapping. Others paid their bribes and expenses with "merchandise" (i.e. cocaine or heroin), or unable to push drugs into the United States, they increased distribution in Mexico where profits were lower but easier to obtain. Gradually—first along the frontier with the United States, then in cities throughout the country—more and more Mexican nationals, especially those under thirty years of age, became regular drug users.

The rivalry among drug organizations intensified in Ciudad Juárez, Chihuahua, which since the 1940s had been the principal pass-through point for goods flowing both north and south across the border. The city doubled in size every four or five years, with marginally serviced *colonias populares* spreading across the desert bordering the Rio Grande (called the Río Bravo in Mexico). During prohibition, night clubs—many quite luxurious—bars, and brothels operated twenty-four hours a day. Some closed after the repeal of prohibition, but the "City of Sin" bloomed again during World War II. Its red light district drew thousands of military and civilian visitors, particularly from overflowing army bases like Fort Bliss just outside of El Paso, Texas.

The "anything goes" and "whatever you want you'll find it here" permissiveness that the city offered was webbed into its political and social life. It was prone to violence even before the arrival of the organized drug exporters. The violence increased with the influx of hundreds of thousands of emigrants intending to cross into the United States and with exorbitant amounts of cocaine and heroin pushed towards the border by those associated with the

Cali and Medellín cartels in Columbia. By the 1990s, murders, assaults, and disappearances were daily events.

Hundreds of young women, the majority students and *maquiladora* workers, were sequestered, raped, and murdered, crimes the authorities never solved. Newspapers including the *El Paso Times, Ahora* of Ciudad Juárez, and international wire services published a seemingly unending series of reports of assassinations, assaults, and disappearances; the victims included soldiers and police as well as rival drug organization members.

Gradually, the principal criminal organizations gobbled up smaller local operatives. ("Join us or join those in the cemetery.") The smaller criminal bands paid monthly quotas to be allowed to operate, and the dominant corporations paid quotas to government officials, business executives, and military commanders and purchased major sports franchises, legitimate businesses, and invested in the stock market.

It was obvious to many of us who live in Mexico that the drug corporations took full advantage of the 2000-2006 Vicente Fox administration's *laissez faire* attitude that everything was right with the world and the country's wealthiest citizens should get to amplify their earnings and power however they could. Informal agreements seemed to have been reached between the federal government and the major drug organizations that each would let the other prosper without interference.[70]

The financial fluidity acquired by the drug corporations enabled them to establish "nations within the nation," which functionally were self-governing and absorbed or supplanted many social and communal activities. Residents of Sinaloa and the adjoining states described networks of citizen espionage that reported every movement of the police or the military and performed many

---

70 Fox and many of his close associates, including his wife Martha Sahagún and her children, accrued immense wealth during his six-year term. In 2009, his former public relations chief, Rubén Aguilar, suggested that the Calderón government work out accords that would allow one or more of the drug corporations to operate without confrontations or further expansions of their territories, further stimulating belief that the Fox administration had engineered such accords while he was president.

auxiliary services, from providing clandestine warehouses, to organizing fiestas that members of the drug organizations attended. Similar networks existed in a number of other states.

A small business owner, an expert in installing and repairing aircraft communications equipment, confided that he knew from the price and upkeep of the planes that some of his clients brought him that they were used by drug organization magnates, "but I had no proof, and I was afraid to go to the authorities because they probably were involved with the *capos.*" His wife, who managed her husband's firm's finances through the travel agency she owned, explained that in Tamaulipas, where they lived, the drug organizations were interwoven into every commercial and social activity. Because the drug organizations had more "*lana*"[71] than the government (money being equivalent to power), they had gained control over everything.[72]

The principal Tamaulipan organization, the so-called "Cartel del Golfo" headed by Juan García-Ábrego, fought intrusions from other drug corporations, particularly those from Sinaloa who were trying to move into cities on the Mexican side of the border, creating the first of many multi-sided conflicts where individual organizations not only battled federal and state authorities but also each other. García-Ábrego was the principal Mexican *capo* with Colombian connections, and transferred thousands of tons of cocaine that had been flown to clandestine landing strips in Quintana Roo and the Yucatán and transported to Matamoros and Reynosa for smuggling into the United States.

When Mexican authorities arrested and extradited García-Ábrego to the United States in 1996, his organization foundered, and its new leaders temporarily allied themselves with the Sinaloenses. Such "marriages" and subsequent breakups occurred frequently throughout the 1980s and 1990s depending upon arrests, betrayals, governmental changes, and business opportunities. But

---

71 Literally, the word translates as "wool," but colloquially is used to indicate money.
72 Interview in Mexico City in March 2008. The person interviewed declined to have his name published for fear of retaliation.

although the names and faces changed, the business continued unabated.[73]

2

In many aspects (investment, trade, communication, transportation, defense) the "nations within the nation" that the drug corporations formed paralleled the structure of Mexico's federal government. Many who operated within the corporate systems of the drug organizations functioned in similar capacities within federal and state law enforcement and within financial entities. The *capos* contributed to local and regional political campaigns, thus assuring themselves of being able to extract needed favors and permissions from the many officeholders in their debt. According to a retired state employee named Pedro Enrique Martínez, who chauffeured a number of Sinaloa politicians,

The *capos* (drug lords) realized it wasn't cost effective to have to keep bribing those who held higher offices, so they started recruiting young local candidates, helping finance them to win elections. Soon, every city, every *municipio* (county), every state bureaucracy was infiltrated. Sometimes the *capos* would go years and not require anything, then one day they'd say, "We need this bill passed" or "We need this shipment to go through," and they'd get what they wanted.

What the leader of the so-called "Sinaloa cartel," Joaquín ("El Chapo") Guzmán, wanted, he informed the Mexican president Felipe Calderón, was to be allowed to run his business without interference from the military, who he said his organization respected.[74] Although some members of the bureaucracy and Senate and Assembly quietly supported this concept, harking back to the

---

73 Francisco Cruz, *El Cartel de Juárez* (2008).

74 In May 1993, the Arellano-Félix brothers apparently attempted to assassinate El Chapo but mistakenly killed Cardinal Juan Jesús Posadas-Ocampo at the Guadalajara airport instead. Federal authorities bungled investigation of the crime, perhaps instructed to do so by the drug organization, and the details about what actually happened remained controversial.

presidency of the PRI's Carlos Salinas de Gortari between 1988 and 1994 when drug exportations enriched the executive without arousing bloody criminal confrontations, Calderón and his administration remained committed to U.S.-financed policies of militarized action.[75]

By then—2008—it was too late to exterminate the drug organizations with military sweeps and street warfare. The buildup of power that had begun half a century before not only had solidified the corporate structure of the drug organizations, but had seduced a significant percentage of the Mexican political system. Throughout the country, politicians and officeholders linked to the dominant political parties were serving two masters, often giving preference to what had become the stronger and wealthier system: that of the drug exporting corporations.

El Chapo made it clear that his "Sinaloa cartel" had no interest in supplanting local or state government. They simply wanted to conduct their business without interference, and their business was drug exportation and sales, not government. Nevertheless, his corporation—like most entrepreneurial businesses in the world—invested a great deal of time and money to suborning those in authority and to influencing political decisions.

Although Calderón and his inner circle were loath to admit it, the militarization provoked greater violence and bloodshed without diminishing the flow of drugs northward (and rapidly increasing narcotics use and addiction in Mexico).[76] As proof of the success of the military operations, Calderón cited increases in the street price of cocaine in the United States, but he did not mention how much those increases stimulated distributors to greater activity. If one examines the prices that cocaine sales

---

75 These U.S. policies included the so-called "Plan Mérida" that dispatched US$1.3 billion in helicopters, arms, and detection equipment to Mexico's federal government in 2009.

76 Gustavo Castillo García "Cae 50% la erradicación de cultivos de cannabis en 3 años," La Jornada, December 26, 2009.In fact statistics reveal that production of both marijuana and adormidera increased during the first three years of militarization, and convictions and destruction of growing areas fell to almost half of what they had been before 2007. La Jornada, December 26, 2009.

garnered in 2009, it becomes easy to understand why traffic increased despite the mobilization of the Mexican military. The following is a chart outlining pricing:

Price for purchasing one kilo of cocaine in February 2009 in:

Colombia	$2,500 (U.S. dollars)
Panama	$4,000
Guatemala	$6,000
Mexico	$16,000
The United States	$27,000[77]

Sold by the ounce in the United States, a kilo of cocaine purchased from one of the estimated 1,500 Colombian "mini-cartels" for US$2,500 would net US$140,000—fifty-six times more than the initial investment.[78] Multiply the US$140,000 by the 1,000 pounds to several tons of Colombian cocaine that the major drug organizations were handling every week, and you're looking at one of the most profitable businesses in the world.

Major media in both countries stimulated reader interest with lurid accounts of ambushes, assassinations, and perceived threats, many of which were fed to them by government sources. In her "Americas Program Column" in March 2009, Laura Carlsen warned that "the language of exaggerated threats infantilizes society with fear as it clears the way for militaristic, patriarchal measures."[79]

It also mythologized how those drugs—principally cocaine and marijuana—were used and sold. Addiction and crime associated with drug users certainly was a major problem in the United States, but the vast majority of users—like the vast majority of persons who buy and use alcoholic beverages—were not addicts.

---

77 Expat Chronicles, May 13, 2010 quoting sources that indicated that from harvest to final sale, the price of cocaine increased 200 percent.

78 Gustavo Castillo Garcia, "El terror marca la vida cotidiana en Reynosa; el narco decide todo," *La Jornada*, March 2, 2009. Various estimates indicate that it cost the drug organizations between 30 and 40 percent of the street price to purchase, transport, and sell the product.

79 Laura Carlsen, "Drug War Doublespeak," Center for International Policy, March 9, 2009.

Bankers, politicians, athletes, university professors, insurance salespersons, construction workers, and thousands of others relaxed or stimulated their senses with various types of narcotics. Many indulged only on weekends, before retiring at night, at parties, or as sexual provokers. They purchased the cocaine and marijuana from other athletes, salespersons, bankers, etc. who had regular suppliers, most of whom they'd been doing business with for years. All were far removed from street warfare between *mafiosos* and armed military, and they are a primary reason that the War on Drugs hasn't reduced the demand for cocaine, marijuana, and other narcotics in the United States.

In her "Americas Program Column," Laura Carlsen insisted,

Drug-war doublespeak pervades and defines the U.S.-Mexico relationship today. The discourse aims not to win the war on drugs, but to assure funding and public support for the military model of combating illegal drug trafficking, despite the losses and overwhelming evidence that current strategies are not working.[80]

As Mexican government emphasis on social and agricultural programs decreased (along with funding for education and health care), more and more people lost faith in those controlling the country's destiny and ignored or tacitly supported the various drug corporations' formation of nations within the nation. At the same time, rivalries among the leading drug corporations escalated. At war with each other, and with federal and state law enforcement, they developed military-like combat organizations instead of merely assembling police-like protection groups.[81]

---

80 Ibid.
81 National security specialist Ghaleb Krame explained that the *narcotraficantes* developed a sophisticated counter-intelligence system and utilized highly mobile guerrilla groups that constantly changed their bases and personnel while the Mexican army, bogged down by traditional channels of protocol and information, was unable to effectively counter these maneuvers. (Francisco Gòmez, "Càrteles adoptaron la guerra de guerrillas,"

After escaping from the Puente Grande prison in 2001, El Chapo Guzmán wedged his way into an alliance with the Beltrán-Leyva brothers' Cartel del Golfo, breaking a duopoly between the latter and Vicente Carrillo's Juárez corporation. El Chapo, the Beltrán-Leyva brothers, and several other drug corporation leaders planned and carried out the assassination of Rodolfo Carrillo in September 2004 and launched a campaign to break up another rival corporation that was headed by the Arellano-Félix brothers in Tijuana. The assassinations of Rodrigo Carrillo and Ramón Arellano-Félix and the arrest of his brother Benjamín disabled both the Tijuana and Juárez corporations' activities in Sinaloa, leaving El Chapo virtually in total control of drug trafficking on Mexico's west coast.[82]

In 2008, El Chapo and the Beltrán-Leyva brothers broke their alliance after Mexican authorities arrested one of the Beltrán-Leyva brothers, and the Beltràn-Leyva gunmen killed El Chapo's son, Edgar, during a Culiacan shootout. In true Machiavellian fashion, El Chapo and the Valencia brothers, who dominated drug traffic in the state of Michoacán, joined forces while the Golfo corporation and the militarized Zetas aligned to dominate activities in northern and eastern Mexico.

As a result of these conflicts, the major corporations wound up with better equipped and better trained units than the federal government, stimulating it to make greater investments in the police and military and cut back social services.[83] At the same time, it expanded its dependence on paramilitaries to do what the police and military couldn't do legally.

According to Mexican psychotherapist Irma López, whose clients included victims of drug negotiation violence, government commandoes participated in—or instigated—confrontations between rival drug corporations. They had the authority to "take out" specific individuals identified as

---

El Universal, January 2, 2010)

82 Ricardo Ravelo, *Herencia maldita* (2007). Contains a detailed account of these mergers and confrontations.

83 Ricardo Ravelo, "Nuevos feudos para el narco," *Proceso,* June 15, 2008.

members of these groups without going through conventional channels.[84] They also infiltrated various drug organizations (and other branches of the government); many of them wound up being double agents, providing information about drug organizations to the government and about government activities to the *capos*.[85]

Their undercover operations were not confined to infiltrating and investigating drug corporation activities, but like the *brigadas blancas* of the 1960s-1970s, they actively disrupted social protest movements and sequestered and sometimes tortured those defending ecological, communal, or union rights. Some human rights advocates insisted that the War on Drugs was actually "a simulation whose real objective is to stomp out growing social discontent" in the country.[86]

Other clandestine forces, primarily formed of former military and police personnel, became the private armies contracted by individual entrepreneurs. These well-equipped and quasi-legal bodyguards escorted dignitaries and their families, guarded business and industrial sites, and, like the drug organization paramilitaries, served as armed couriers. They operated with the knowledge and consent of federal, state, and municipal law enforcement. As an Oaxacan self-employed contractor, Ali Jiménez told me "It's come to the point that the government lets these guys (entrepreneurs) surround themselves with gunmen since nobody can trust the police, and there's no public security."

Although during Bush's second presidential term the United States was already deeply involved in financing the invasion of Iraq and the conflict in Afghanistan, it

---

84 Under PRI administrations in the 1970s and 1980s, so-called Brigadas Blancas ("White Brigades") conducted secret anti-guerrilla activities that resulted in hundreds of disappearances and incarcerations in clandestine prisons.

85 Although the following lacks official confirmation, a Mexico City journalist described during an informal "charla" a "quadruple agent," who the government was paying to infiltrate one of the cartels, the cartel was paying him to infiltrate a rival cartel that was paying him to infiltrate the federal prison system.

86 Miguel Badillo, "Oficio de Papel," *Noticias, Voz e Imagen de Oaxaca,* December 29, 2008.

determined to augment its attempt to reduce drug importations with a "Plan Mexico" similar to the "Plan Colombia," which had dispatched U.S. troops and military hardware to that South American country. Mexican authorities zilched the "Plan Mexico" nomenclature and insisted that no U.S. troops be actively included in the so-called drug war; consequently, "Plan Mexico" was renamed "Plan Mérida," a cosmetic change that private school educator José Gutiérrez called "a bit of nationalistic showboating designed to demonstrate how firmly Mexico could deal with the *pinches yanquis*."[87]

Final authorization of Plan Mérida was delayed in the U.S. Congress until requirements for Mexican government accountability, which included dealing with corruption and improving the rate of convictions and reducing escapes and releases from incarceration because of legal technicalities, were approved. In announcing the involvement of the military in the War on Drugs, President Calderón described it as a "temporary" measure, perhaps to lessen criticism of his sidestepping Mexico's constitution in order to authorize it.

But the expenditures required prompted many Mexicans to question how temporary the maneuver was intended to be. Plan Mèrida included no mention of efforts to reduce drug consumption in the United States, and little publicity was given to the fact that it called for expenditures of US$7 billion of Mexican government financing in addition to the US$1.5 million in helicopters, detection systems, and military hardware the United States would provide.

For a country that has 60 percent of its citizenry living in poverty—20 percent in abject poverty—US$7 billion is a huge expenditure and necessitated diverting funds from other sources—particularly education and agricultural support. And where was the seven billion going to be spent? With U.S. firms, of course.

Also not included in the plan was mention of private arms sales by U.S. dealers to the drug corporations, which prompted observers south of the border to note that Plan Merida escalated the battles between two U.S.-equipped

87 Telephone conversation, March 2008.

antagonists rather than attempting to solve problems generated by violent competition among exporters. Although stricter regulations against money laundering were inaugurated in both Mexico and the United States, they did little to dismantle the financial networks operated by the drug corporations or reduce their economic support of politicians and legitimate businesses.

President Calderón boasted that his administration's focus on military confrontation was breaking up the cartels and that the increased number of deaths reflected the military's success in hunting down and arresting drug corporation leaders. But national security experts like Eduardo Buscaglia insisted that the militarization affected only the outward aspects of the problem and did not thwart internal corruption or political protection of the drug corporations.[88]

When Calderón's government refused to negotiate with El Chapo, the latter let it be known that his organized and efficient combat force would retaliate immediately and brutally to the arrests or slayings of members of his organization. Although he claimed to have "respect" for the military, he announced that he held local and state police in contempt. So many of them were pocketing money from competing drug corporations, that internecine warfare erupted among various municipal, state, and federal contingents. Various police detachments became victims of rival drug corporation assaults for having supported activities of one of their competitors.

Throughout the first three years of Calderón's presidency, assassinations of police commanders and police detachments multiplied. Gunmen attacked police garrisons near Acapulco, Guerrero, several times in 2006 and again in 2008; ambushes and raids erupted in other states, including Nuevo Leon and Baja California. The state of Chihuahua's police force became so decimated by

---

88 Eduardo Buscaglia, interviewed by Ricardo Ravelo, April 19, 2009. Buscaglia indicated that the country might finally respond effectively when "the violence of the *narco* knocks on the door of [Mexican entrepreneurs] Carlos Slim, Salinas Pliego or Azcárraga Jean" and they realize "that the cost of not doing anything is higher than the cost of taking action."

killings and desertions that recruiters could no longer find Chihuahuans willing to fill the vacancies and scoured the poverty-riddled states of Oaxaca and Chiapas for recruits.

Calderón and his advisors turned deaf ears to complaints from various state governors and municipal leaders who criticized military interventions and who cited statistics that indicated drastic increases in assassinations and corruption despite troop deployments and campaigns to purge local mayors and other officeholders accused of having drug organization connections. In the words of a former Chihuahua journalist (who left the profession because of death threats), "It [the War on Drugs] is like a football [soccer] game without coaches or referees, soldiers and narcos charging this way and that, doing more harm to the spectators than to each other."[89]

3

Unlike the drug corporations that had infiltrated all levels of government and whose payrolls included thousands of lookouts, messengers, farmers, and truck drivers, the federal government and the inexperienced Mexican military seemed to lack cohesive intelligence reports or effective plans for doing more than random searches and seizures. Often they responded to misleading or false information they acquired from informants, many of whom were paid by the drug organizations to finger competitors or businesses whose only connection with the *mafiosos* was having failed to pay adequate protection money. The amounts that the drug corporations, like the Cartel del Golfo, were able to pay seduced even high-ranking members of Mexico's top organized crime-fighting agency, SIEDO (Sub-Prosecutor General of Special Investigations into Organized Crime).

The federal Attorney General's Office (which had its own problems with infiltrators in its ranks) investigated high-ranking SIEDO functionaries in 2008—investigations that were hampered because the Cartel del Golfo was being

---

89 E-mail correspondence, May 2007. He wishes to remain anonymous for fear of retaliation.

informed of every step that the PGR (Prosecutor General of the Republic, Mexico's Attorney General's office) took from SIEDO informants, some of whom were receiving more than $Mex450,000 a month from the Beltrán-Leyva *capos*. Finally, through a former Cartel del Golfo member who testified against the organization as a protected witness, the PGR arrested Sub-Prosecutor Noé Ramírez-Mandujano and Miguel Colorado, SIEDO's coordinator of intelligence, for their connections with organized crime.[90]

As El Chapo and other *capos* promised, the drug corporations retaliated for police arrests or betrayals.[91] In May 2007, gunmen assassinated José Lugo, Mexico's coordinator of information of the Center for Planning and Analysis to Combat Organized Crime. Others ambushed and shot Edgar Millán, acting head of Mexico's federal police, later that same year. In 2008, the Cártel de Juárez announced the sentencing to death of twenty-one anti-narcotics agents that it accused of crimes against the organization. They demonstrated their "nation within the nation" authority by tracking down and executing four of the twenty-one within days after the announcement.

In November 2008, a drug organization hit squad abducted and executed Army General Mauro Tello a few days after he assumed the post of anti-drug czar in Cancun, Quintana Roo,[92] and in 2009, they executed Édgar Enrique Bayardo-del Villar while he was breakfasting in a Mexico City Starbucks coffeehouse. Bayardo-del Villar, a former PFP comandante, became a government protected witness after revelations that he was being paid US$25,000 monthly by El Chapo's Sinaloa cartel.

In May 2009, over 200 federal agents stormed a house in Cuernavaca, Morelos, that reputedly belonged to Alberto

---

90 Ricardo Ravelo, "Golpe fallido no era 'El Borrado,'" *Proceso,* May 24, 2009. Another, who was arrested during "Operation Limpieza" in December 2008, was Arturo González-Rodríguez, member of the elite Presidential Guard.

91 They issued the same threats to rival organizations, creating Hatfield-McCoy feuds that took 7,000-15,000 lives a year.

92 Tracy Wilkinson, *Los Angeles Times,* "Ex-general, 2 others found shot to death near Cancun," February 4, 2009.

Pineda-Villa, one of the Beltrán-Leyva brothers' top operatives. Pineda-Villa wasn't at the family reunion being held there; nevertheless, the federal police arrested everyone at the celebration, including Pineda-Villa's aged mother and father.

To justify their actions, the *federales* forced those netted in the sweep to pose holding AR-15 automatic rifles, which were allegedly found in the residence but were later determined to have been planted there by the arresting police. According to reportage of the incident by the magazine *Proceso,* the huge *narcomantas* (banners hung by the drug organizations to publicize accusations and events that government-aligned media refused to report) that appeared throughout Mexico in reaction to the arrests of innocent family members "struck fear" into the members of the president's Federal Security cabinet.[93] And although Calderón's government tried to squelch rumors that the fatal crash of a Learjet carrying Government Secretary Juan Camilo Mouriño wasn't the result of pilot error, journalists and commentators throughout the country insisted that the government version was a cover up and the aircraft had been sabotaged by El Chapo's corporation in retaliation for the arrest and imprisoning of one of his top aides.

As the competition among the major drug organizations increased, with break-offs considered treasonable and the assassinations of rival leaders commonplace, the militarized "Zetas" emerged as an elite armed force, first aligned with the Beltrán-Leyva Gulf Cartel, then as an independent corporation functioning on both Mexico's northern and southern borders. The Zetas were tightly disciplined (their leaders were deserters from Mexico's Special Forces and many had been trained by the U.S. School of the Americas and/or the Kaibilies in Guatemala); they openly recruited active duty militaries to the desert. (Mexican authorities confirmed that nearly 30 percent of Mexico's active duty enlisted force deserted before completing their enlistment, a clear indication of how

---

93 Ricardo Ravelo, "En Cuernavaca, golpe fallido," *Proceso,* May 24, 2009.

successful recruitment by the Zetas and other drug corporations had become.)[94]

Although the Zetas occasionally openly confronted police and military units, they focused primarily on intimidating and extracting quotas from growers and transporters as well as those engaged in legitimate businesses, including cattle ranchers, merchants, local entrepreneurs, bar and nightclub owners, farmers, *polleros*, and truckers. They dealt harshly with those who tried to circumvent or reduce these obligations, kidnapping, torturing, and often decapitating those who were delinquent in their payments.

Chihuahua state official Guillermo Ramírez countered suggestions that the Zetas tortured their victims before killing them (and sometimes dissolving their corpses in acid or incinerating them in 200-liter tanks of burning diesel oil) out of sheer beastliness by affirming, "No, they have a reason for everything they do." That the victims were tortured, often for several days or weeks before they were killed, spread fear among even persons who might risk being assassinated for failure to conform, he insisted.[95] So successful (and so notorious) did the Zetas become, that smaller criminal groups throughout the country and in the United States called themselves Zetas, making the compact, militarily organized group seem larger than it actually was.[96]

---

94 Fox News Latino, April 18, 2012. Desertions totaled 106,000 between 2000 and 2006.

95 Guillermo Ramírez, e-mail communications between February 2009 and April 2009.

96 *Al Jazeera*, "México in the Crossfire," March 29, 2009 (online version). The Zetas organized their units in groups of thirteen "hawks" (i.e. privates), who reported to one "central" (i.e. sergeant), who in turn reported to those above him. As in the other drug corporations, the "hawks" conducted twenty-four hour surveillance of key communication points and the activities of rival corporations, the police and the military. The hawks reported suspicious activities, and in March 2009 they kidnapped and decapitated a military intelligence officer who was prying into their activities.

Many of these criminal activities had little or nothing to do with the drug trade, although, media reports linked them to the criminality that enveloped Mexico.

"Simply stated, the drug dealers kill and rob each other, the police and soldiers kill and rob us," a pre-school teacher named Mónica Figueroa attested while I was conversing with her and her husband. Although both admitted that was an exaggeration, the intent of her message was clear: One doesn't have to deal with the drug organizations; police and soldiers are much more difficult to avoid.[97]

Al Jazeera's "Mexico in the Crossfire" reported 7,000 drug organization slayings between January 2008 and January 2009.[98] So frequent had these killings become that by 2008 Mexican newspapers like *La Jornada* grouped daily execution and assassination reports under a single back page headline. During the first eight months of 2009, they reported an average of twenty-one killings a day, some committed by and some committed against the military.

Although media reports made it seem that the entire country was in turmoil, with turf wars and military interventions endangering lives and property, the vast majority of the country's residents only connection with confrontations came through reading newspapers or watching television. The northern and northwestern states were most affected by the violence, but even there, Rotarians went to their meetings, fans flocked to see soccer teams like the Tecos, Chivas, and Diablos Rojos compete, children endured school, and families gave their fifteen-year-old daughters elaborate *quinceñerias*—coming out parties. Inflation and employment were much more provocative issues than drug-related crime for most citizens.

---

97 Stout, "Land of Job," *Social Justice Review*, October 2009. Refer to source for a more detailed account of events.

98 *Al Jazeera,* "Mexico in the Crossfire," March 29, 2009. Although *Al Jazeera* exhibits an editorial bias when reporting Mideast events, its coverage of Latin America is not affected by regional political concerns like most accounts published by U.S. and Mexican media. Mexican government statistics listed the 2008 toll at 6,290, including military and law enforcement.

Nevertheless, as profits from the exportation of drugs to the United States continued to soar, reaching a confirmed thirty billion dollars a year by 2008, the drug corporations were able to shrug off interceptions and confiscations by law enforcement and the military and hire tens of thousands of military deserters, returned or deported emigrants, and unemployed and underemployed young men and women, thus continually strengthening their control over police and government officials.

By 2008, Mexico had committed some 70,000 troops (including militarized police and not-yet-graduated military cadets) to the War on Drugs. Because it had been a peacetime force primarily involving garrison duty (and since 1994 containment controls around the Zapatista autonomous communities in Chiapas), the Mexican military offered relatively few benefits and minimal salaries to enlisted personnel. Recruiting was focused on marginal residents of city slums where life was hazardous, choices were few, and anything seemed better than remaining in the barrios.

Theoretically, recruits needed to have completed junior high school to enter the military, but proof seldom was required, and criminal records, if confined to misdemeanors, were often overlooked. These ghetto-bred soldiers, many just out of basic training, adhered to medieval practices of supplementing their meager salaries with what they could acquire during *cateos* (searches and seizures of property) and shakedowns.

Victims accused soldiers of stealing money, jewelry, cell phones, and laptops during searches and of stripping personal property from persons stopped at highway checkpoints. In September 2009, Gustavo de la Rosa, of the Chihuahua state Commission on Human Rights, sought asylum in the United States after receiving death threats from unidentified persons who told him to stop criticizing human rights violations by the military and to cease defending victims of military aggressions in Ciudad Juárez.[99] Federal authorities consistently derailed prosecution of soldiers accused of abuses by insisting that

---

99 "Se refugia en Texas defensor de los derechos humanos," *La Jornada,* October 1, 2009.

those levying the charges "are politically motivated" and the accusations were exaggerated or falsified.

Like the military, the drug corporations recruited from marginal areas. Although they promised "guns, money, cars, and women" to potential deserters, many of the hundreds of thousands they hired did not carry weapons and primarily acted as lookouts, messengers, decoys, and money handlers. Like many legitimate corporations, the drug organizations established salary scales, usually beginning with the equivalent of US$800 per month, a figure that doubled after a set number of months or year of service. (Schoolteachers in southern Mexico receive US$900-$1,100 per month; most workers are paid less, thus vaulting a newly recruited drug corporation lookout or messenger into the upper 10 percent of money earners in his or her community.)

By 2009, distrust of the government had become the norm throughout Mexico. "When a government lies to its people, the people lose faith in that government," Ugo Codevilla told an Oaxaca book presentation audience in January of that year. Not only do citizens lose faith in the government, but in the entire social and political system within which that government operates. In Mexico that included the media, the Catholic Church, and, in many people's minds, the United States, which for over half a century had functioned as a safety valve for Mexico's economy.

To tens of thousands of young people, employment with a drug corporation "at least offers something," a seventeen-year-old, high school dropout told me after a friend offered to connect him with a recruiter.

"I could never go back to making ten dollars a day," *Al Jazeera* quoted a drug organization member. "At least here I get paid, and I have some opportunity to rise up. In other jobs, I will always be at the bottom."[100]

Throughout Mexico, drug corporation units maintained twenty-four-hour-a-day monitoring of major highways, airports, and police and military movements. Those employed in these activities were not the snarling, dripping-with-blood, gun-wielding gangsters so often

---

100 *Al Jazeera*, "Mexico in the Crossfire," March 29, 2009.

depicted in the U.S. press and cinema. Many were employed as janitors, watchmen, vendors, and day laborers and reported to their supervisors by cell phone, usually referring to the police and military as "the family," "the neighbors," or "the workers."

Each used only a *mote* ("nickname") and knew his or her supervisors by *motes* as well, making it difficult for the authorities to trace chains of command since those in the lower levels of the organization didn't know the actual names or backgrounds of those to whom they reported. That most of these newly recruited members of the corporations had no criminal records and intermingled with the general population created an environment "like those old science-fiction movies about androids, you never know who's on your side and who isn't," a Mexico City journalist told me.

Like other major drug exporting corporations, the Zetas's network included police officers and state and federal officials throughout the areas they dominated. "Textbook military intelligence," Guillermo Ramírez noted, "if the Federal Police were one-tenth as thorough, they could have made hundreds of arrests and saved thousands of lives."[101]

But the federal government, headed by President Calderón and his ultra-conservative National Action Party, lacked the top-to-bottom cohesion that the PRI had manifested during its seventy-year control of finances and policy. Although PAN held the presidency from 2006 to 2012, it lacked a majority in the Senate and House of Deputies and only controlled one-third of the governorships, including several in states reputedly dominated by "narco politics." Because he needed—or thought he needed, or his party thought that he needed—the support of those governors Calderón shunted aside, revelations about narco-business connections concerning PAN and PRI governors and congressional lawmakers, whose support gave PAN a majority in the legislative bodies.

---

101 Guillermo Ramírez, e-mail communications between February 2009 and April 2009.

Consequently, prosecution of commerce in cocaine, marijuana, and other drugs occurred in a patchwork pattern with political alliances given priority over enforcement. Many governors, high-ranking politicians, business impresarios, and generals remained immune even when military raids or PGR investigations targeted their agencies. The one governor who was prosecuted and sentenced to prison, Mario Villanueva of Quintana Roo, insisted throughout his imprisonment that he was arrested and prosecuted because he refused to grant multi-billion dollar concessions to relatives of President Ernesto Zedillo.[102]

The state of Quintana Roo hugging the west side of the peninsula of Yucatán virtually did not exist as part of the Republic of Mexico until Cancun and the surrounding area, including Isla Mujeres and Cozumel, developed as tourist attractions. A territory throughout the eighteenth and nineteenth centuries, Quintana Roo achieved statehood in 1974. Except for the touristed areas with their pristine beaches and five-star accommodations, the rest of the newly formed state was virtually unexplored and provided ample sites for the construction of clandestine airstrips for South America-originated flights bearing cocaine to be smuggled into the United States.[103]

With the construction of the landing strips, the major drug corporations' presence on Mexico's southern borders with Belize and Guatemala increased dramatically. The interconnections among exporters, transporters, and purchasers grew more complicated, and the transfer points, routes, and the involvement with police, *aduanas,* and legal services underwent constant changes. The fact that the *capos* were operating in their home territory and the Mexican military was not gave the former the flexibility

---

102 Ricardo Ravelo, *Herencia maldita* (2009).

103 Belice, the former British colony that borders Quintana Roo on the south, also hosted these flights. I was impressed during a 1980s visit there by new highways that seemed to lead nowhere, constructed as many U.S. highways were at the time with luminous disks along each shoulder. Later I learned that the highway served as a landing strip for twin-engine Cessnas hip-hopping north from Colombia and Venezuela through Panama with cocaine to be pushed through Mexico.

to counter raids and interventions. As greater evidence piled up to demonstrate that military sweeps, *cateos*, and takeovers increased rather than diminished the violence associated with the drug trade, journalists, academic investigators, and government officials advocated changes in the management of the War on Drugs.

Only when "the structure of power that those controlling the politics of the nation have maintained as accomplices and members of this series of criminal organizations has collapsed" will real solutions be possible, Guillermo Garduño-Valero, a specialist in national security analysis from Mexico's Metropolitan University, told *La Jornada*.[104] The drug corporations had become so powerful politically, he argued, that both the federal and state governments had become subservient to them, and despite occasional arrests and assaults on organization leaders, they had diminishing influence over the lucrative trade.

4

Throughout Mexico, the various drug corporations developed "safe cities" in which cooperative authorities sanctioned the transference of their product to points further north. Cuernavaca, the capital and principal city of the tiny state of Morelos just south of Mexico City, had a lengthy history as one of these safe cities.

PRI governor Armando León Bejarano fled in 1983 after a judge filed an order for his arrest for tax evasion from "illegal enrichment," ostensibly originating with drug corporations that his government sheltered. Federal prosecutors and local and foreign journalists accused one of his successors, Jorge Carrillo-Olea, of protecting both the Cartel de Golfo's Amado Carrillo (no relation to the governor) and the *capo* of the Juárez Cartel, Juan José Esparragoza, during the late 1990s.

Federal organized crime investigators targeted Carrillo-Olea's successor, panista Sergio Estrada-Cajigal, and his

---

104 Alfredo Mèndez, "Al narco se le mantiene y protege desde el poder, asegura especialista en seguridad," *La Jornada*, March 2, 2009.

connections with drug organizations but did not press charges, because the 2000-2006 Fox administration apparently wanted to avoid the bad publicity that accusing a governor from their own party would evoke. (Estrada-Cajigal was also allegedly involved romantically with Esparragoza's daughter.)[105] As a result, the federal government wound up tolerating Estrada-Cajigal's impunity just as he tolerated the presence of the drug corporations, a pattern repeated throughout Mexico that allowed the *capos* and their minions to expand and grow more powerful with what amounted to government permission.

In December 2009, federal marines raided the luxury condominium in which Arturo Beltrán-Leyva was living and killed the Gulf Cartel *capo*. The condominium was only a few doors away from the *Palacio del Gobierno* (the governor's palace) and very close to the home of Governor Marco Adame-Castillo, who apparently knew that Beltrán-Leyva was his neighbor. According to a Cuernavaca language professor, Beltrán-Leyva was anticipating a mealtime visit from General Leopoldo Díaz-Pérez, the commanding officer of the 24th military zone headquarters in Cuernavaca, on the day of the assault.[106]

Newspapers and magazines splayed photos of the bullet riddled and bloody *capo* on covers and front pages, and President Calderón lauded the operation in a prime-time television appearance. He called the only marine killed during the action a martyr and a hero. Gulf and Sinaloa corporation spokespersons responded by announcing that they would retaliate to assassinations of their members by taking the lives of ten persons (soldiers, their families, etc.) for every one of their *compadres* the government killed.

The day following the marine's interment, gunmen broke into his mother's house and murdered her and his sister and brother and aunt. People throughout Mexico questioned whether or not Calderón's need for praise and

---

105 Ricardo Ravelo, "Un golpe lleno de dudas," *Proceso,* December 20, 2009.

106 Telephone conversation, December 2009. The professor was repeating information that had spread through Morelos after the assault but never has been officially confirmed.

publicity as a crime fighter had set up the retaliation killings since the president had not only identified the marine but also his hometown in the state of Tabasco.[107] Calderón condemned the butchery but insisted "my government" would not be intimidated by "criminals without scruples" and would continue to use all the force available to it to submit those involved to justice.[108]

Between 2000 and 2010 the governments of Mexico and the United States justified military actions and portrayed the War on Drugs as a battle between good and evil with no gray areas in between. In many respects, this duplicated U.S. rhetoric about "defending our borders" from terrorists and illegal entrants, specifically Mexican nationals seeking work in the United States.

To make the rhetoric effective, it was necessary to villainize the so-called perpetrators of the "evil" and to ignore the dominant reasons that the evil existed, which were consumption of marijuana and cocaine in the United States and agri-business and industry's need for cheap labor. Although many Mexican government spokespersons (and many journalists and academics) insisted that the problems involving drug exportations and emigration originated north of the border, and Mexico was an innocent victim forced to follow the dictates of their powerful neighbor, they failed to mention how deeply rooted Mexico's economic and social systems were in inequality and massive poverty that triggered the migrations northward and fed the drug trade.

U.S. distributors obtained their cocaine and heroin through connections with Mexican exporters, but, for the most part, were handling small quantities that could be moved more discreetly than the large amounts passing through Mexico. Although payoffs to law enforcement and customs personnel occurred north of the border, U.S.

---

107 Numerous observers, including award-winning journalist Miguel Ángel Granados-Chapa and Catholic Bishop Raúl Vera-López, criticized the marine assault to kill Beltrán-Leyva instead of capturing him and extracting information concerning the drug corporation's operations and its connections with law enforcement and political figures.

108 "Asesinan a familiares del marina muerto en operativo contra Beltràn-Leyva," *El Nuevo Diario*, December 22, 2009.

dealers lacked the corporate structure that the Mexican exporters had built up. The major profits—and consequently major battlegrounds—existed in the importation and cultivation of narcotics, transporting it through Mexico into the United States and getting it into the hands of U.S. distributors. Doing so created large scale —and very costly—logistical needs that included airplanes, high speed launches, armament, and bribery, elements that were not essential in the United States.

Many of the groups that received and distributed the narcotics in the United States were linked to specific Mexican corporations just as U.S. auto, livestock, cosmetics, and computer exporters were linked with importers in Mexico. Gangs in the United States clashed primarily over obtaining drugs for street sales, but the majority of imported narcotics passed into the hands of white collar distributors with regular clients who could afford the prices established for purchasing cocaine and other drugs.

Although journalists and editors would like to deny it, newspapers and television profit more from graphic reports about beheadings, drug raids, and high speed chases than they do from features about controlled or casual use of narcotics. Attitudes towards drug use in both countries run a gamut between "drugs are a sin" to "I enjoy them, why not?" That they can be detrimental to one's health, just as the consumption of alcoholic beverages, cigarette smoking, overeating, driving a car at excessive speeds, or long-term exposure to direct sunlight can be detrimental, is grounded in fact.

Unfortunately, facts and politics don't go hand in glove. Nor do facts and marketing. Newspaper wire services and television reports designed to stimulate interest and sell sponsors' products (and/or comply with ownership political biases) influence public opinion and public opinion influences the decisions of legislators and congressmen. As Laura Carlson insists:

These claims and others like them, although unsubstantiated, accumulate into a critical mass to push a public consensus on implementing dangerous and delusion policies ... Like the model it mimics—the

Bush war on terror—the drug war in Mexico is being mounted on the back of hype, half-truths, omissions, and outright falsehoods.[109]

Government sources on both sides of the border denied that U.S. military intervention into Mexican territory was being planned; nevertheless, several governors of states on the U.S. side of the border urged the federal government to provide permanent military protection. Residents of Texas's Rio Grande Valley reported "constant movement" of military-type vehicles, plans for National Guard mobilization and an increase in vigilante propaganda and recruitment during the last years of the Bush administration and first years after Barack Obama became U.S. president.[110] However, statistics from U.S. cities bordering Mexico did not show increases in major crimes despite the turf wars south of the border.

5

Major questions that needed to be answered were shunted aside by policymakers on both sides of the border, and preference was given to partisan stances that had less to do with the drug trade or the war against it than they had with maintaining economic and political power. Neither government seemed capable of asking whether Mexico could really afford to end the production and exportation of heroin, cocaine, marijuana, amphetamines, and designer drugs without its U.S.-dependent economy collapsing.

---

109 Laura Carlson, "Drug War Doublespeak," March 9, 2009.
110 Conversations with residents from McAllen, Mission, and Harlingen, Texas, during 2008 and 2009 and e-mail correspondence from various immigration and civil rights activists, including Henry Saunders. Saunders pointed out that those benefiting most from the threats of drug violence spreading northward were gun manufacturers and military contractors whose lobbyists were urging greater exportations to Mexico and more aggressive defense installations on the U.S. side of the border.

Severing this source of income, when an estimated 78 percent of the money moving through Mexico's banking and commercial systems originated with the drug trade, would be catastrophic. Even though many within Mexico's financial system—both governmental and private—were aware of the country's dependency on money derived from the narcotics trade and what could happen if it suddenly were cut off, they withheld this awareness from public consumption, preferring to emphasize the criminality of the drug corporations and the need to combat organized crime.

The drug organizations operating in Mexico exemplified what "free enterprise" is about: developing and marketing a product that satisfied willing consumers. Their armed components made their competition more deadly than those experienced by competitors in other industries, but their methods of operation duplicated those of legitimate corporations: They sought (or bought) government support, networked a well-organized retail trade, and invested their profits in condominiums, the stock market, and high-visibility, consumer items. Their corporate structures, departmentalized into distinct operations and with well-defined chains of command, enabled them to replace any executive who was arrested or killed without that individual's loss materially affecting production or sales.

The money they brought into Mexico, unlike money brought in by legitimate corporations, did not require government investment and consequently was untaxed and unreported (which prevented it from benefiting the nearly 60 percent of the population with inadequate and/or poverty level incomes). Nevertheless, what the *mafiosos* spent on purchases, construction, and salaries circulated throughout the economy. The owner of a Michoacán *taquería* reflected the viewpoint of many Mexican residents: "They have *lana*, they eat well; I now have five locations instead of just one."

Both Mexican government officials and private economists and sociologists discussed the legalization of some or all drug use. Proposals to decriminalize the possession of small amounts of marijuana, as various states in the United States had done, came under discussion during the early years of President Vicente Fox's administration but evoked a vehemently negative response, particularly from the Catholic Church hierarchy and those influenced by Church doctrine. Calderón's PAN government seemed more inclined to reinstitute the Salinas de Gortari era of tacit coordination with a single dominant drug corporation and eliminating its competitors by force, a process that could not be discussed openly and would have involved purging local, state, and federal governments of alignments with everyone except the chosen affiliate (which many sources in Mexico insisted was El Chapo's "Sinaloa cartel").

The hype given to the War on Drugs and the ongoing assertions of its success made such a maneuver impossible, unless it could have been done surreptitiously and with a certain amount of cooperation from U.S. agencies, such as the DEA. Reducing assassinations and gun battles among rival groups (included branches of law enforcement) could have lessened media focus on the dangers of living in and traveling in Mexico, but it also could have created a situation similar to what happened in Colombia after the breakup of the large cartels in the country.

Instead of three or four major groups competing to dominate production and export, the Colombian drug corporations splintered into hundreds of independent organizations, many with specialized functions such as cultivating, processing, transporting, or exporting.[111] This diversion made military intervention ineffective; no matter how many *mini-cartels* the armed forces waylaid or destroyed, countless others existed to replace them.[112]

As long as the assassinations, beheadings, *cateos*, and corruption of government officials remained south of the border, the United States was able to maintain its pro-military stance, send money and arms to Mexico's conservative government, and close its eyes to the cost in human lives. Mexico, on the other hand, rejecting any form of legalization, remained bound to its U.S.-appeasing commitment to continue a confrontation that offered no

111 Ricardo Ravelo, *Herencia maldita* (2009).
112 Yahoo! Voices, "The New Face of Colombian Drug Trafficking,"
April 26, 2010.

hope of a prompt solution. Even though the War on Drugs had failed to do more than aggravate crime—including acts committed by the police and the military—there seemed no choice but to continue and hope that the United States could somehow alleviate a situation that many Mexicans accused it of perpetrating and for which it lacked either the experience or the resources to effectively culminate.

Isolating the War on Drugs as a regional problem distinct from worldwide social and economic situations and unrelated to other issues between the United States and Mexico simplified propaganda (and consequently simplified congressional attitudes and activities) but doomed the militarized attempts to failure. Drug use was not confined to the United States nor was the production and dissemination of cocaine and other so-called "illegal substances" merely a U.S.-Mexico dispute. A worldwide market existed; violently repressing the supplying of the product to purchasers who wanted it, escalated crime rather than reducing it.

The international market weaved suppliers with consumers through banking and investment systems that involved the production, supply, and purchase of thousands of other goods and services, including oil and natural gas products, food and grains, communications systems, and sports franchises. The drive to open markets for exportation simultaneously opened borders for the entrance of workers, drugs, and lifestyles. Isolating a single aspect—drugs, immigration, tourism—created a fiction for which the solution became another fiction. But the lives being lost were real.

Although legalization would have re-channeled importation and sales and made addiction, overdoses, and side effects a public health problem instead of strictly a law enforcement concern, drug-related crimes would have continued to exist, just as alcohol-related crimes continued to make headlines and fill jails after the repeal of prohibition. Taxes on importation and sales could have financed rehabilitation and other government programs (or "stuffed more into the pockets of the politicians!" cautioned Carlos Santiago, a high school teacher involved in anti-government protests), and purity and dosages could have been regulated by health or pharmaceutical authorities.

Corporations handling importation and sales could have been effectively audited, but social, ethical, and religious conflicts over morality and behavior would have continued, as would conflicts about age restrictions, distribution points, price regulations, and sales locations. Those opposed to drug use still would have been opposed to it and closet users still would have indulged surreptitiously.

Legalization in itself would not address or resolve the economic issues that gave rise to the complex business of drug exportation and use. Legalization would have to occur in both Mexico and the United States simultaneously to be effective. By the same token, restricting or controlling the financing of drug operations would not be possible without breaking up the distribution and investment chains that involve not only the two governments, but entrepreneurs and legalized businesses as well.

The nationalism exhibited by the governments of both the United States and Mexico impeded dealing effectively with drug cultivation and distribution. Coupled with the lack of accurate information—and/or falsification of the information available—it created a paradigm where the solution preceded analysis and wrenched fact and fiction into a definition that fit the solution, rather than the solution being the culmination of analysis. In much the same way that trying to solve the "illegal immigration problem" by constructing walls and making arrests put the cart (solution) before the horse (employers), trying to curb the importation of cocaine, marijuana, heroin, and other drugs by militarized procedures was doomed to fail, because it did not recognize or deal with the undiminished demand for the products involved.

Left unresolved, or left with the inadequate solution of military campaigns against those producing and distributing what a worldwide market desired, the War on Drugs threatened the stability of Mexico's conservative government, prompting it to concentrate more power in the hands of fewer participants and encouraging it to extralegal assassinations, *cateos*, and financial consolidations. This, in turn, aggravated already dangerous social conditions, triggering increasingly aggressive and violent public protests, greater emigration, and more pervasive institutional corruption. That both countries were content to consider the drug trade as unconnected with emigration/immigration, increased poverty, and the insertion of multinational corporations into Mexico's political and economic life resulted in innumerable deaths, displacements, and the consequent misery of millions of people involved.

SECTION III – POPULAR PROTEST

1

Struggles reawakened and stomped down have been a twentieth century-Mexico scenario. The most prominent uprisings—the student-led protests in Mexico City in 1968, the Zapatista rebellion in Chiapas in 1994, and the university strikes in Mexico City in 1999-2000—forced the country's centralized government to make changes, many of them cosmetic and others later abrogated, but did not alter the neo-liberal "democracy" that had impoverished the vast majority of the country's residents while enriching a small coterie of entrepreneurs and transnational mega-firms.

Neither the Mexican government nor the government of the United States took the victims of social repression, of the War on Drugs, of the mistreatment of immigrants, of human rights abuses, or of poverty into account when economic, territorial, and political decisions were made. Both governments seem to forget that they represented the people but legislated as though government was a private corporation only responsible for its membership. Tensions among the excluded—the majority of the two countries' populations—threatened to surge destructively against those who created or exacerbated the situations in which the societies of the two countries found themselves.

"One of the objectives of the administrators of neo-liberal systems like those in the United States and Mexico is to erase all memory of social struggles," *La Jornada* correspondent David Brooks quoted Noam Chomsky following a presentation by the latter in New York City on June 14, 2009. Chomsky told his audience of 1,500 in the Riverside Church that he detected a latent tendency among those deprived of the wealth that the system had accumulated to renew struggles that "could be reawakened and now is an appropriate moment for that to happen."[113]

According to Chomsky, neo-liberal economic philosophy masquerading as "democracy" spread the costs of generating income among the masses but funneled the profits into the hands of a wealthy minority. Although he was speaking globally, he was accurately describing twenty-first century Mexico. PRI administrations from 1982-2000 attempted to cloak the process that Chomsky described, but the PAN governments blatantly rewarded a select few and drove millions into poverty, increasing emigration and opening channels for drug corporation *capos* to flourish.

The governmental structure instituted after Mexico's internal revolutions of 1910-1926 facilitated adoption of neo-liberal values. The constitution of 1917 established strong executive powers to which the legislative and judicial branches were secondary. The resultant one-party system created a well-remunerated Senate and House of Deputies to rubberstamp presidential actions and vote against any attempts by popular movements to abrogate their interests. After the election of Miguel de la Madrid in 1982, Mexico's neo-liberal presidents reversed the direction taken by Lázaro Cardenas (1934-1940), who had strengthened infrastructure and promoted industrial development. Under the neo-liberal presidents, industrial and agricultural development took a back seat to the exportation of raw materials, particularly oil.

The PAN administrations beginning in the year 2000 consolidated control of public opinion through a duopoly granted to the two major television operatives, Televisa and TV Azteca, who also controlled the majority of large-circulation newspapers and virtually all radio outlets. PAN deferred tax payments to major corporations, including trans-nationals, and removed subsidies from gasoline and electricity. Even after the financial collapse of 2007-2009 PAN pushed privatization of public functions, including health services, social security, primary and secondary education, and government daycare centers. Systematically

---

113 David Brooks, "El neoliberalismo, raíz común de las crisis actuales," *La Jornada,* June 15, 2009.

raised taxes placed increasing financial burdens on the struggling middleclass.

Chomsky revised the nineteenth century dictum "an intelligent minority has to govern an ignorant and meddlesome majority" by substituting "an elite technocracy" for "intelligent minority," but he insisted that the same motives—enrichment of the few at the expense of the many—guided the neo-liberal oligarchs just as they had nineteenth century financial barons.[114] Control of this "ignorant and meddlesome majority" in Mexico necessitated repression of mass movements, including those originating with labor unions, curbing education, and supplanting indigenous culture with a media dominated "reality show" that exalted consumerism and only peripherally discussed poverty, un- and under-employment and social issues, thus creating an impassable *barranca* between the politics of the few and the majority of the population.

This substitution of participatory government by a state-controlled *telenovela* also keyed Mexico's international relationships, even with countries and agencies that were able to see through the sham. One of the most critical of these agencies, Amnesty International, repeatedly admonished President Calderón's PAN government for failing to acknowledge and respond to human rights violations cited by AI's investigations.

"The reports to Amnesty International were part of the charade," insisted former government attorney Andrea García. "They (the government) simply forwarded what had been written as 'goals and procedures' instead of factual information." They made no mention of federal and state government failures to put those goals and procedures into practice and frequently dealt with alleged abuses by noting that they had been received and "acted upon" (the "action" having consisted of reviewing and archiving them).

"Pure and simple fantasy," is how García described both the reports and publicity acclaiming Mexico's progress concerning human rights issues.[115] Mexican officials

---

114 Ibid.
115 Andrea Garcia, interview by Robert Joe Stout, September 15, 2009.

continued to list reforms and new programs without mentioning what steps were being taken to implement them.

Amnesty International insisted that the Mexican government hadn't, but was obliged to, investigate and act upon hundreds of assassinations and disappearances that occurred during the *guerra sucia* ("dirty war") waged against supposed guerrilla groups and individuals during the 1960s and 1970s. AI also detailed unresolved federal police and military abuses (including torture, robbery, rape, and arbitrary detentions) in 2006 during armed interventions to crush popular protests in San Salvador Atenco, in the Estado de Mexico, and in Oaxaca, and failures to recognize or prosecute offenses by the Mexican military against the civilian population during the War on Drugs. The international organization's secretary general, Irene Khan, called Mexico's attitude towards human rights "schizophrenic." Journalist Ricardo Rocha insisted that she applied the label, "with good reason, we fight for human rights in the exterior, signing whatever treaty is put in front of us, while we stomp on those same principles inside our frontiers."[116]

Other violations concerned repressive treatment of Mexico's *indigena* population, harassment and arrest of human rights advocates, arresting journalists who reported government cover-ups, and failures to investigate and prosecute crimes against women. Government Secretary Fernando Gómez-Mont defended military personnel after the slaying of two innocent children in June 2010 and, previously, the assassinations of two university graduate students in Monterrey by charging human rights investigators with bias. Oaxaca governor Ulisés Ruiz blatantly rejected AI's documentation of assassinations, disappearances, and beatings in 2006 by joking "they read like they were written by the APPO" (the initials of the Peoples' Popular Assembly of Oaxaca).

Summarizing AI's documentation, Rocha insisted, "If those in power evidence a lack of respect for human rights,

---

116 Rocha Ricardo, "Mexico blamed," *Noticias, Voz e Imagen de Oaxaca,* August 10, 2007.

it creates a pernicious and corrosive impunity that corrupts the entire governmental apparatus."[117]

The failure to investigate human rights offenses by the Mexican government and the consequential assumption of power by drug lords and regional caciques prompted journalists and academics to describe the country as an *"estado fallido"*—a "fallen state." According to them, the adoption of and insistence on neoliberal economic patterns had undermined the country's ability to be self-sustaining and had led to an almost complete dependence, financially and socially, on the United States. U.S. backing (if not generating) of the country's internal politics, particularly the War on Drugs, was thrusting the country deeper and deeper into poverty and more stridently under military control.

Journalist and environmental activist Gustavo Esteva asserted that those formulating U.S. policy towards Mexico were well aware of President Calderón's "lack of legitimacy and his incompetence" and were motivated more by domestic politics and national security than by imperialistic domination.[118] As I've pointed out in Section I and in *Why Immigrants Come To America,* U.S. policy had never been focused on choking off undocumented migration, but on keeping the need for the continuing supply of minimum- and less-than-minimum wage workers underpublicized while responding to individual complaints about immigrants and their activities.

Esteva contradicted the "fallen state" belief by asserting that corrupt or incompetent governments can ruin a country's economic well-being when its institutions "produce the opposite of what they try to do ... Instead of protecting the citizenry the state security apparatus has dedicated itself to spying and repressing it in order to protect the government and its institutions."

During the 1960s, a Mexican secret service officer told me "disappearing someone is a tremendously effective tool" for controlling group behavior. Not that he advocated it, he insisted, but he explained that unlike arrest or assassination, making someone "disappear" aroused

---

117 Ibid.
118 Gustavo Esteva, "Nuestros fracasos," *La Jornada,* April 20, 2009.

uncertainty in those associated with him or her. It made them feel impotent and lessened attempts for revenge by establishing a "gray world" of promises, hope, and denial.

Amnesty International cited over 700 unresolved "forced disappearances" related to the *guerra sucia.* Government investigations yielded few confirmable facts, although individual ex-soldiers testified that they saw (or participated in) the dumping of manacled prisoners out of helicopters and airplanes into the Pacific.

The student riots in Mexico City in 1968 altered government control of news and criticism; as a result, disappearances as a means of intimidating political dissidents diminished. But throughout the latter part of the twentieth century, they continued sporadically, the most notable cases being those of two members of the EPR (Ejército Popular Revolucionario) in Oaxaca and persons associated with Zapatista and anti-mining and anti-clear cutting activities in the Estado de Mexico, Guerrero, and Veracruz.[119]

After federal troops and federal police swept members of the People's Popular Assembly, passers-by, and shoppers into prison without allowing them to consult lawyers or relatives in Oaxaca in 2006, I questioned a state government attorney, "What if most of them are innocent?"

"All the better," he responded, "it will make the rest of the people more afraid."[120]

2

In 2009, Mexican journalist Luis Hernández-Navarro perceived "discontent breaking out on all sides like the

---

119 Carolina Gòmez Mena, "Rosario Ibarra," *La Jornada,* April 20, 2009. Senator Rosario Ibarra de Piedra, whose son was among the *desaparecidos* during the *guerra sucia,* insisted in 2009 that the number of disappearances had increased dramatically since President Felipe Calderón took office in 2006.

120 Some of those arrested and flown to the San José del Rincón federal prison in Nayarit, several hundred miles northwest of Oaxaca, reported that their captors laughed and taunted them, "We're going to dump you in the ocean and no one will ever know what happened to you!", apparently the fate of many of those who disappeared during the *guerra sucia.*

bubbles in a vat of water about to boil." Frustrated by police corruption and increasing crime, residents of city barrios took matters into their own hands, apprehending supposed criminals and battling the security forces that attempted to rescue them. These included attempted lynching and community attempts to free persons that police had taken into custody on disputed charges, residents blocking highways to keep trucks from entering recently reopened mining operations and *campesinos* forcing wind-generated energy operations to shut down, because the foreign owners had fraudulently obtained the land on which they constructed the huge wind machines.

The wives of miners killed during a massive cave-in at Pasto de Conchas, Sonora battled police who tried to remove their barricading of the mine entrance, and federal police pistol whipped women trying to block trucks hauling toxic waste to a newly opened dump in the state of Hidalgo. Workers cheated of promised wages attacked the facilities of their employers in various parts of Mexico, including Veracruz and the Federal District, and students at several national and state universities closed their campuses because of cutbacks in degree programs and the curtailing of scholarships.

By the beginning of the twenty-first century, over 80 percent of Mexico's population lived in urban areas disconnected from traditional communal roots. Emigration to the United States had become a way of life for millions of men and women. These two factors—urbanization and migration—triggered a dramatic increase in the number of single-parent families and homeless and runaway children. The consequent lack of adequate incomes created what Mexico City priest Father René Jiménez called "a rootless agglomeration of young people who've lost faith in government, society, and religion," which nourished petty crime and gang membership.[121]

Before the massive urbanization of the last half of the twentieth century, most adolescents grew up in communal circumstances surrounded by relatives and peers who created networks of inclusion and sharing, "cushions against misery and loneliness" that did not exist in less

---

121 Conversations in Mexico City in June 2009.

organized, urbanized environments of absent or single-parent households, overpopulated barrios, and criminal gangs.[122] By 2010, joining a gang was easier than migrating (where one would also be criminalized for being what one was: poor, uneducated, abandoned, the product of a broken home).

Blogger Jorge Zepeda-Patterson described a Federal District fourteen-year-old who, like millions of other Mexican adolescents, "came to the conclusion that the only way not to be beaten and assaulted was to join a gang...." To do so he "simply had to comply with the conditions of initiation: rape a woman and kill a rival, which he did."

The drug corporations in Mexico absorbed hundreds of thousands of these adolescents every year. Most of them felt they had so little to live for that they feared neither imprisonment nor death. Contrary to the stance of the Catholic Church hierarchy, they hadn't lost faith; how can one lose something one never had? Having never received respect or love, millions of teenagers in Mexico lacked respect for others and lacked the ability to love. A Sinaloa seventeen-year-old told me, "Life is short so you get what you can while you can."

Belonging to a gang or a drug corporation provided identity and belonging. So did being part of an organized social protest. Among the most vigorous and loyal members of Oaxaca's Popular Assembly were junior high and high school dropouts, street kids, graffiti strikers, teenaged day laborers. Though not previously politicized, they knew and understood better than many of their working and middle-class companions what conditions actually existed in Oaxaca and who was imposing them.

The People's Popular Assembly of Oaxaca burst into being in less than a week after armed police unsuccessfully attempted to break up a camp-in by striking schoolteachers (Section 22 of the national teachers' union) in May 2006. The teachers' yearly contracts had terminated, and the union demanded that the state and federal governments reclassify their salary base, which would have raised the minimum wage to workers throughout the state. The union rejected a state offer to

---

122 Jorge Zepeda-Patterson, www.jorgezepeda.net.

fund a portion of what it would cost to effect the reclassification and made good their threat to take over the city's Zócalo and adjoining Alameda.

They filled some fifty blocks in the heart of the city with tents, huts, tarpaulins, spouses, dogs, and children. Businesses throughout the central part of the city closed, tourists cancelled hotel reservations, and bus and auto traffic ceased or had to be diverted to other parts of the city. Oaxaca's governor Ulisés Ruiz responded by ordering the state and municipal police to clear the strikers out. A primary school teacher who was in the Zócalo on June 14 remembered that "The helicopters came in so low their big rotors sent things flying through the air. Then the whistling sounds as they fired tear gas. We were coughing and choking, we were blinded, people were shouting for their children. Then the police came, swinging their clubs, smashing everything."

Despite the tear gas, a majority of the teachers clustered into resistant groups and fought back, hurling bottles and paving stones, swinging mop sticks, chairs, tent poles, belts, and rebar. Others commandeered city buses and forced the police to scatter as they accelerated towards them. By 9:30 the entire force of over 1,000 police had evacuated the area. *Noticias*'s correspondent, Pedro Matias, called the victory "a parting of the waters." Oaxaca, he prophesied, "never will be the same."[123]

What had begun as a legal sit-in, overnight became a massive resistance movement. The representatives of over 300 separate organizations talked, urged, argued, and convoked their first reunion on June 20 and announced the formation of the People's Popular Assembly of Oaxaca (the APPO). Participants included *indigena* federations from throughout the state, radical student and youth groups that espoused revolutionary overthrow, human rights organizations, and many Catholic priests. Teenaged gang members joined dozens of other organizations flocking to support the teachers, as did a congregation of women students, housewives, and working women who formed

---

123 Matias made the statement during an appearance before the Rights Action Emergency Human Rights delegation, of which I was a member, in December 2006.

their own contingency—the Coordinadora de Mujeres de Oaxaca (COMO)—within the APPO.

"Mexico winning the World Cup couldn't have generated more enthusiasm than that first assembly!" a delegate named Cabrera told me.[124]

The Popular Assembly became a permanent organization despite assassinations, disappearances, and arbitrary arrests. During 2006, paramilitaries in Oaxaca killed between twenty-three and twenty-six protesters, including U.S. Indymedia photographer Bradley Will. Pressured by the U.S. government to resolve Will's slaying, Oaxacan authorities arrested one of Will's companions, ignoring video evidence that showed four gun-wielding paramilitaries charging Will's barricade seconds before he was shot.

The Mexican Attorney General's representatives bungled the investigations by mislabeling and losing evidence, and Oaxacan authorities charged potential witnesses with "withholding evidence" thus nullifying any testimony they could have given. Oaxaca governor Ulisés Ruiz's attorney general's office refused to free the man they'd accused and ignored protests from both U.S. and Mexican citizens and citizen groups.[125] Ruiz and representatives of President Calderón insisted that they would not negotiate with "lawbreakers and criminals," even though appeals courts determined that the charges filed against those involved in the sit-ins lacked validity.

Rather than negotiate with the protesters, state and federal agents infiltrated the movement. Three of them, posing as Popular Assembly participants, poured muriatic acid on the transmitters of Radio Universidad, the station that had been broadcasting news, warnings, and

---

124 Robert Joe Stout, "No End in Sight," *The American Scholar,* spring 2008. See article for more details.

125 The accused man, Manuel Martínez-Moreno, was arrested nearly two years after Will's slaying and was a victim of international politics as well as law enforcement fraud. Because of upcoming state and national elections, some members of Ulisès Ruiz's government felt that protests against his imprisonment would be less damaging to the PRI than admitting that he was innocent, thus opening the door to protests about corruption and/or paramilitary kidnappings and assassinations.

instructions to the thousands of protesters who had occupied the city's central business district and who had set up nightly barricades throughout the city to prevent incursions from *escuadrones de muerte* (death squads). Some for whom the government had filed arrest warrants fled the country; others "went underground," as one of the young women involved in the takeover of commercial radio stations told me.

Those who didn't go underground faced constant and often brutal harassment. Three weeks after a November 2006 assault by over 4,000 federal police and military to break up a march and drive the Popular Assembly out of Oaxaca, four men armed with high-powered weapons leaped out of a pickup and dragged Assembly spokesman Florentino López and two companions out of their car. He told the Rights Action Human Rights Delegation:

> They threw me on the pavement face down and stepped on my head. They handcuffed me and wrapped a whole lot of adhesive tape around my eyes ... they threw me in the back of the pickup, they laughed at me, they mocked me, they banged my head against the truck bed. 'We need to wipe you out,' they scoffed.

> I thought they might be drunk the way that they acted. I was sure they were going to kill me. They stopped at a house. I heard them address someone at the door as 'Colonel,' then heard someone ask, 'Is the airplane ready?' and I thought they were going to fly me away, like they did the others [who were apprehended on November 25].... They beat me and pressed a pistol again my head and each time I answered 'no' [to questions about Assembly activities] they kicked and hit me.... They insisted that I tell them who paid me, how I supported myself, and when I answered honestly they said I was lying.... I don't know how many times they pushed me down, then grabbed me back up. They were pissed off, they threatened to hang me.

López testified that his assailants identified themselves as the *escuadrón de muerte"* and finally dumped him and his two companions, who'd also been beaten, on a deserted road outside of the city.[126]

He wasn't the only *escuadrón de muerte* victim. Nor the only victim among anti-government protesters. Armed guards shot and wounded a protester outside the hotel that the governor supposedly was visiting. Snipers executed a mechanic who had been instrumental in distributing anti-government propaganda during a protest march. Administration henchmen, apparently non-uniformed police, yanked journalist Pedro Matias out of his car and threatened to rape and kill him for articles he'd written. Non-uniformed police also sequestered university student Francisco García after he'd left the Assembly's radio station, beat him, threatened to rape his *novia*, and accused him of theft.

During Ruiz's six-year governorship, Oaxaca's state government neither charged nor convicted any police, military, or paramilitary for any of the crimes reported by the civilian population.

"The government's intention literally was to chop off the heads of the movement," Diego Enrique Osorno wrote in *Oaxaca Sitiada*. "They accused everyone they detained [on November 25 and 26] of damage to personal property, arson, sedition, kidnapping, criminal association, rabble rousing and mutiny, charges for which they never were able to provide proof but that didn't matter, it wasn't necessary."[127]

A similar type of justice was levied against the purported leaders of the uprising in the rural community of San Salvador Atenco in the Estado de Mexico. The scene of massive protests against evictions to construct a new airport, which the federal government reluctantly abandoned during the administration of Vicente Fox, San Salvador Atenco surged back into the spotlight in May 2006 when hundreds of citizens swarmed after police attempting to break up and arrest flower vendors they charged with invading public right-of-way.

---

126 Florentino López, testimony given to the Rights Action emergency human rights delegation, December 2006.
127 Diego Enrique Osorno, *Oaxaca sitiada* (2007).

Federal reinforcements firing tear gas and wielding batons crushed the "rebellion" and arrested dozens of protesters. Disregarding testimony from Atenco citizens (including videos taken during the suppression), the presiding judge sentenced the protest leaders to the maximum prison terms permitted by Mexican law. Authorities did not investigate or prosecute the rapes of seven women by federal police during the repression.

Political science professor Victor Raúl Martínez-Vásquez linked their aggression with the repressions in Oaxaca six months later.

> The severity of the penalties puts in evidence the vengeance that economic and political forces whose interests were affected by the tenacious resistance shown by the *campesinos* to prevent their lands from being used for the construction of a new airport in the city of Mexico's metropolitan zone.[128]

Over four years after the federal police assault on Atenco, Mexico's Supreme Court ordered the release of the Atenco leaders, ruling that the evidence presented against them was too flimsy to support guilty verdicts. Several months earlier, the same court ordered the release of twenty-nine paramilitaries convicted for the assassinations of more than forty pro-Zapatista *indigenas,* the majority of them women and young children, in Acteal, Chiapas, because of "irregularities" in the prosecution process.[129]

As Mexican presidents had done since the founding of the republic, Vicente Fox and Felipe Calderón utilized the PRI pyramidal structure that extended to regional strong men and caciques to retaliate against social or political protesters. Assailants associated with the government or

128 Victor Raul Martínez-Vásquez, "Atenco," *Noticias, Voz e Imagen de Oaxaca,* November 23, 2009.

129 Television newscasts by both Televisa and TV Azteca applauded the paramilitaries' release and criticized their convictions "without proper evidence" as concessions to foreign human rights advocates. Neither the federal government nor private investigators have been able to confirm who ordered the pogrom or whether, like the assault in Atenco, it was intended to serve as a warning to those who might stand up against government dictates.

government-supported caciques assassinated over twenty anti-administration activists in Oaxaca between 2006 and 2009. Hired *porros* (political henchmen) and paramilitaries in the state of Guerrero killed or "disappeared" over 200 members of the emerging PRD as they tried to proselyte membership in rural areas between 1989 and 1996.

None of the crimes were thoroughly investigated, and no convictions resulted.[130] Nor were charges brought against the caciques that controlled illegal clear-cutting operations in the state of Campeche. After unidentified assailants killed two federal inspectors there in 1996, the federal government suspended foresting inspections in what it defined as "places of risk."[131] Abuses and unresolved crimes prompted many Mexican citizens to believe that police, police acting as paramilitaries, or federal agents were behind most of the assassinations and forced disappearances. Residents of many communities considered law enforcement personnel to be threats rather than protectors and reacted violently against intrusions.

For over half a century guerrilla and supposedly guerrilla "armies" had appeared in the rugged mountainous areas of Guerrero, Oaxaca, and the states that bordered them. Only the Zapatistas in Chiapas achieved a measure of success, but the constant military presence surrounding them limited their political and economic influence after 1994. The Popular Revolutionary Army (EPR) operating clandestinely in Guerrero and Chiapas issued threats and recriminations, but in their only overt attack, they sabotaged several Pemex pipelines in 2007. Shortly afterwards, federal officials arrested two of their leaders, Edmundo Reyes and Gabriel Cruz. The government refused to acknowledge their whereabouts, and the two men were never seen again.

The IRC's Kent Paterson insisted that the "drug war serves as a convenient cover" for repression against protest

---

130 Kent Paterson, "Mexico's New Dirty War," http://americas.ircnline.org/am/6714, April 5, 2010.

131 Often, the owners of the companies doing the unlicensed clear cutting were prominent contributors to political campaigns (or even held political offices) and had much more influence than those protesting timber cutting on communal lands.

organizations and named farm protest, anti-kidnapping, indigenous rights, and human rights advocates, as well as street vendors, gay and women's rights, and anti-clear-cutting activists among the victims.[132]

"One doesn't know who's on who's side," a young university student named Guillermo Ruiz told me in 2009. "The police belong to the gangs, gang members to the police, guerrillas to both. You never know who you're talking to. Even the *campesinos* fight against each other. Mexico's a no man's land."

When the People's Popular Assembly in Oaxaca took a stand against government aggression and demanded the resignation of Ulisés Ruiz as the state executive, it advocated non-violent reforms and a people-centered horizontal political system. Despite the police and military assault to drive the Popular Assembly out of Oaxaca, over 10,000 protesters forged through the streets of the city six weeks later, a movement that "demonstrated that inconformity is alive and well, that the causes for protests are legitimate and that Oaxaca cannot continue to be hostage to pretenses, lies, illegality and injustice."[133]

Nevertheless, deprived of its ability to occupy physical space and suffering the loss of its communications systems, the loosely formed union of many disparate organizations came apart at the seams. Many segments pulled away to renew local or less ambitious projects. A section of the dissident teachers established a separate union (with federal acknowledgment and support) and several of the more militant groups split away to function independently, although some like the Popular Revolutionary Front (FPR) continued nominally to be part of the assembly.

The leaders of the FPR never publicly acknowledged that their organization was a political front for the EPR, but journalists and political observers noted a strong connection between the two organizations. Since its formation in the 1980s, the FPR had a strong presence in

---

132 Kent Paterson, "Mexico's New Dirty War,"
   http://americas.ircnline.org/am/6714, April 5, 2010.
133 Ernesto Reyes, "Escenarios del movimiento popular Oaxaqueño" in Carlos Beas, *La batalla por Oaxaca,* 2007.

Oaxaca; the governments of both Ulisés Ruiz and his predecessor, José Murat, imprisoned several of its members.

National Marxist-Leninist Communist Party leaders prophesied that Oaxaca was merely the first surge of a movement that eventually would overwhelm the status quo and credited the Popular Assembly with providing the model for subsequent uprisings. "Oaxacanize" emerged as a governmental term to describe the amalgamation of protest forces and the threats they presented. The military and militarized police stepped in immediately to crush incipient protests, particularly those involving students or *indigenas*.

"The federal government will not stand for another *desmadre* like the one that occurred in Oaxaca!" student leader Luis González reported being told after heavily armed federal police overwhelmed normal school students who'd begun a protest over job placements in Guerrero.[134]

"Oaxaca," priest Manuel Arias insisted, "has set an example for the rest of Mexico and that example will go forward. This is what scares the [federal] government the most."[135]

La Jornada's Julio Hernández told a March 2008 Día de Mujer forum in the city of Oaxaca, "What happened here is an example, an example of action ... that gave hope to the entire pueblo of Mexico." He affirmed that the Popular Assembly's takeover of government functions "awakened a sleeping giant" and sparked an immense empathy throughout Mexico and great hopes for its success.

Oaxaca journalist Pedro Matias countered assertions made by Ruiz and by Calderón's former government secretary, Francisco Ramirez, that the assembly was funded by revolutionary elements and outside agitators.

---

134 From a free broadside distributed in the city of Oaxaca.
135 Statement made during a meeting with members of the Rights Action Emergency Human Rights delegation, December 2006. See Stout, *"Desmadre," Global Politics,* spring 2008, for more detailed coverage. "APPO," derived from the Popular Assembly's initials in Spanish, was a term often used to describe the group and its participants.

"What's supporting the APPO? Poverty stricken people, that's what!"[136]

Priest Manuel Arias added, "It's a lie that money is behind the movement. What's behind the movement are *viveres*—food and water—that the people lack, that the people need."

3

As more and more Mexican citizens perceived that the *patrón* (father, cacique, governor, or president) no longer deserved unquestioned obedience, the crack that had begun to appear in the deeply ingrained paternalism that dominated the country's political system grew wider. Similar to what happens when a son or daughter rebels and the paternal authority responds by becoming more dictatorial, Mexico's authoritarian leaders increased repression of protest movements and narrowed their social and political vision to "obey or else" dictates that ignored the problems created by crime and increased poverty and inflation.

Citizens from all walks of life, feeling abandoned by the father figure who was supposed to take care of them, stopped responding to its dictates. The law belonged to whoever dared to implement it—*Zapatistas,* drug corporations, criminal gangs, popular assemblies, *indigena* pueblos. Several national surveys revealed that police— along with politicians—rated among the least trusted professions, often ranking lower than *ambulantes,* smugglers, and prostitutes. That they protected those in power rather than the people oppressed by them prompted communities to form vigilante movements rather than respect authority. A fracas that erupted in Tochmatzintla, Puebla, in March 2009 was typical.

Whether the three state police sent to Tochmatzintla fired at someone or were firing in the air wasn't determined, but within minutes nearly 3,000 men, women, and teenagers converged on the astonished authorities,

---

136 Pedro Matias, appearance before the Rights Action Emergency Human Rights delegation, December 2006.

disarmed them and locked them in the town jail. Hundreds surged forth shouting "Lynch them! Lynch them!" Even after the arrival of nearly 200 armed state and federal agents, the town's residents refused to release their captives, who apparently had come to arrest three locals for an alleged assault.

The townspeople countered law enforcement threats with, "We have guns; we'll fight back!" and insisted that they were going to keep the captives under guard unless there were lawyers present to verify the conditions of their release. After a two-day standoff, the state government complied and the vigilantes freed the three officers.[137]

A similar fracas erupted six months later in Santiago Tolman in the Estado de Mexico when two state police pulled up in front of a primary school and corralled a student just as he was leaving class, apparently to interrogate him about one of his professors. People from the neighborhood poured out to rescue the student; others rushed to church to clang the parish bells. Before the two officials could drive away, they were overwhelmed by over 500 townspeople.

Emergency calls alerted a state anti-riot force that arrived, over 500 strong, two hours later. They attacked the vigilantes with clubs and tear gas and rescued the two police. The townspeople regrouped and counterattacked with clubs and stones and set fire to three police vehicles. One of the townspersons justified their actions by insisting, "We're fed up with the authorities and want them to know that here in Tolman the people are going to take justice into their own hands!"[138]

Towns and villages like Tochmatzintla and Santiago Tolman throughout central and southern Mexico remained tightly unified despite migration and urbanization. Their inhabitants knew each other, worked with each other, intermarried, and most shared the same ethnic and cultural backgrounds.

---

137 Arturo Alfaro Galàn, "Amenazan con linchar a policías judiciales y municipales en Puebla," *La Jornada,* March 27, 2009.

138 Javier Salinas Cesàrio, "Otumba," *La Jornada*, December 9, 2009.

From 1810—the beginning of the revolution against Spain—until after the revolution of 1910, many communities became virtual city-states. These communities, "*autarquías*" ("autarchies") in the words of María Dolores Paris-Pombo, had little or no contact with the federal government and were controlled by local caciques who fought federalization or solidified their regional control by supporting PRI governors.[139]

During the colonial period, Spain forced local caciques to pay tribute to the crown but granted them power to rule without its intervention, a practice that continued through the first century of Mexico's independent rule. The revolutions of 1910-1926 battered but did not destroy this system. Many caciques and ladino landholders supported one or another of the various revolutionary forces and emerged having lost territory but not their governing power. The various indigenous cultures retained their customs, their languages, and, to a large extent, their systems of communal government. Entire generations lived and died without coming into contact with either Spanish or Mexican governing authorities.

Throughout the eighteenth and nineteenth centuries, a so-called "noble elite"—wealthy landholders and investors who separated themselves from the rural *campesino* culture—occupied most of the important governmental posts and controlled commerce and politics. They enjoyed *indigena* festivals, products, foods, and customs but excluded the *indigena* population from participation in government and business dealings. For them "the *indigenas* were a form of animal like horses and goats that neither spoke the official language nor shared their living areas," a participant in the 2007 forum in the city of Oaxaca commented.

"Gone but still imitated," Guadalajara private secretary Adriana Perez described politicians as "more influenced by *telenovelas* than budgets, initiatives or citizen complaints." The separation that existed between the elite and the *proles* during the colonial period continued to exist into twenty-first century Mexico. Appearances, like the following, distinguished office holders and candidates: hair

139 Maria Dolores Paris-Pombo, *Oligarquía tradición y ruptura*, 2001.

styles, imported wine and cognac, silk shirts and kangaroo leather shoes, meals at exclusive restaurants, wives or mistresses who were pop singers, beauty queens and movie stars. "Politics is an exclusive club. And those who were not born into membership put on the most extravagant displays," Perez insisted.[140]

The noble elite's hold on state governments diminished after the Mexican Revolution broke up many of the huge land holdings and the expanding middle class pushed its way into the economy. As members of the newly formed state political party, which became the PRI, they replaced the aristocracy as elected and appointed office holders.

They did not, however, change the system, which was based on the few controlling the many. Everything that took place between the community and the PRI world of autocratic rule went through the PRI politicians, including state and federal financing. Periodic local protests and uprisings erupted but were subdued, and the families in power retained their caciquedoms.

Both the noble elite and their less aristocratic successors maintained close ties with the Catholic Church. Church authority over morality was heavy handed, although the noble elite were accorded a great deal of leeway in both financial activities and personal deviations.

Because Marxist theories and the overthrow of the czars in Russia had influenced the formation of the new Mexican state and the public universities taught Marxism, philosophically and historically if not as doctrine, Catholic bishops and priests told their parishioners that the universities and the intellectuals threatened *"Dios, la Virgen y la Patria"* ("God, the Virgin of Guadalupe and the nation") by promoting "moral outrages" like nudity in art and sexual descriptions in literature. They asserted that the Church and the values it espoused were being persecuted; consequently, Catholics had to defend their faith against deviations from established doctrine."[141]

This traditionalism played to prejudices dating to the previous century when "culture" represented by classical music, art, museums, and philosophy belonged to the

---

140 Adriana Perez, conversations in Oaxaca, December 2009.
141 José Joaquín Blanco, *Un chavo bien helado* (1990).

noble elite that kept the majority of the population immersed in poverty and illiteracy. The Church, a clergyman told me when I was a university student in Mexico City, "is many different things to many different people but is always the same faith." The rich went to their churches, he explained, the poor to theirs, each to deal in their own way with the problems they faced.

Since 1982, when Miguel de la Madrid took office as the nation's first neo-liberal president, the governmental elite endorsed higher education in technical fields, law, and economics while berating student unrest and cutting funds, particularly in the humanities. Politicians encouraged working class and rural voters to view the universities as festering vats of anti-Church atheism and anti-establishment thinking.

While the Church did not openly take an anti-higher education stance, its hierarchy advocated private over public education and tried to promote Catholic teaching in the schools. By aligning itself with the conservative PAN administration, the Church accrued more political clout after Vicente Fox was elected to the presidency in 2000, including a lessening of restrictions against religious participation in politics, property ownership, and religious education imposed by the constitution of 1917. Church authorities successfully lobbied for greater penalties against abortion and same-sex marriages and attributed social unrest and crime to the breakup of the traditional family structure.[142]

Nevertheless, within the Church individual priests and bishops took stands against human rights abuses. Bishops Raúl Vera and Samuel Ruiz openly supported the Zapatista movement, the striking miners in Cananea and Pasta de Conchos, Sonora, and the massive protest in Oaxaca. This accommodating of dissent by the Church paralleled long-standing PRI philosophy by allowing a limited amount of self-expression as long as it didn't directly challenge the

---

142 Both abortion and same-sex marriages were legalized by the government of the Federal District, but the conservative PAN and PRI state governments in the rest of Mexico imposed severe penalties for abortion and failed to uphold laws against gay bashing.

authoritative structure. Individual priests participated in protests and openly criticized governmental actions while the Catholic hierarchy maintained its stiffly traditional and overtly authoritarian posture.

Archbishop Héctor González of Durango ignited a controversy in April 2009 by telling his parishioners that the *capo* of the Sinoloa drug cartel, Joaquín ("El Chapo") Guzmán "lives a little past Guanacevi. Everyone knows this except for the authorities."[143] Durango's governor Ismael Hernández huffily insisted that the archbishop should go to the federal police with this information.

The governor's defense triggered public derision. If everyone in Mexico except the authorities knew where El Chapo lived, the authorities either were lying about not knowing his whereabouts or they were stupider than everyone else in the country. Various people that I talked to asserted that both were true, the majority conclusion being that the federal government was lying and was in cahoots with El Chapo or was afraid of him, but the general conclusion was that the archbishop's parishioners confided in him, because they were afraid to go to the police or distrusted state and federal authorities.

This lack of confidence was not confined to Calderón's National Action Party. Mexico's bureaucracy—not unlike that in contemporary Russia and many other countries in the Western world—sponged reports of abuses into a netherworld of procedures, files and postponements and repression, overt or surreptitious, continued. The Mexico City daily *Reforma* published statistics that revealed that less than 5 percent of reported crimes were solved, and not all of the perpetrators of those crimes were sent to prison.[144] Citizens throughout Mexico refused to report violations, because they became victims of police who threatened them, extorted money from them, or assaulted them.

---

143 Patricia Dávila and Rodrigo Vera, "Iglesia y narco: la confrontación," *Proceso,* April 26, 2009.

144 Victor Raúl Martínez-Vasquéz, presentation of *La APPO,* in May 2009 asserted, "In Mexico 98 percent of the crimes that are committed remain unpunished, particularly for those who apply for stays or who enjoy the protection of the authorities."

Authorities, including President Calderón, manipulated laws to conform to authoritarian programs. In November 2009, the president announced the federal takeover of Luz y Fuerza del Centro (LFC), a governmentally-funded power company that served the central part of the republic. In doing so, he also dissolved the 100-year-old Mexican Electrical Workers Union (SME). Armed federal troops occupied offices and work stations "in the night, like bandits, like cowards!" expostulated SME leader Martín Esparza. The purge thrust nearly 40,000 union workers onto the streets, and the federal government acquired miles of fiber optic cable, which Labor Secretary Javier Lozano indicated would be transferred to private investors.[145]

Prior to the takeover, Calderón's government had attempted to thwart Esparza's reelection as SME president by financing an opposition candidate who accused Esparza of misuse of union funds and fraud.[146] When that maneuver failed, federal authorities liquidated the LFC, citing inefficiency and mismanagement, and turned its operations over to the Mexican Electrical Commission (CME). Armed grenadiers repelled SME union protesters from returning to their work stations or recovering either personal or company equipment. Labor unions, citizen groups, and liberal politicians mounted protest demonstrations and marches, and over forty displaced SME workers launched a hunger strike in Mexico City's Zócalo.

Despite the protests and a partial national work stoppage in May 2010, President Calderón and Labor Secretary Lozano continued their privatization policies, which included abolishing the legality of mining strikes in Cananea and Pasta de Conchos. Armed federal police broke the miners' picket lines and occupied the facilities so

---

145 Patricia Muñoz, Fabiola Martínez, and Alma Muñoz, "Existen condiciones pada llegar a una huega nacional," *La Jornada,* November 12, 2009.

146 Esparza denied the charges, although many journalists and political observers believed they were not entirely fabricated. Subsequent events shoved them out of the spotlight and Esparza became a "champion of the oppressed and disenfranchised," to quote a July 2010 presenter in Mexico City's Zócalo.

Grupo de Mexico owners could reopen mining operations.[147] Meanwhile, the pro-Calderón media ignored heated protests against the unions and their members and focused on bicentennial celebrations and Mexico's national soccer team's participation in World Cup matches in South Africa.

When the International Labor Organization called for a thorough examination of the Pasta de Conchos cave-in and demanded that the Mexican government retrieve the bodies and adequately indemnify the survivors, government officials graciously accepted the ILO's demands, but despite investigations that showed multiple irregularities in the management of the mine, inadequate safety procedures, maintenance and upkeep failures, and the absence of the medical personnel required by law, the only action they took was to file charges against the leader of the miners' union for misappropriation of funds.[148] Efforts to retrieve the bodies of those buried by the explosion were abandoned a few days after the cave-in.

The federal government also declared a twenty-two-month-old miners' strike in Cananea illegal, giving Grupo Mexico the right to end the employment of any union members who refused to go back to work.[149] The Mexican Jurists' Union condemned the government's actions as "arbitrary and illegal" and organized protests against them. In Tijuana, Baja California, representatives of Mexico's government-sponsored national human rights organization tried to prevent a group of Tijuana wives and mothers from processing accusations against the military for the false arrest, torture, and illegal confinement of their husbands and sons because of threats of arrest and death that citizens had received for denouncing violations by the military. Unable to secure representation in Mexico, the group filed charges through the Inter-American Commission of Human Rights.[150]

---

147 Arturo Cano, "Nada de desaloga pacifica," *La Jornada,* June 8, 2010.

148 "Electrical Workers Occupy Zòcalo as Leaders Are Charged," Mexican Labor News & Analysis, August 12, 2011.

149 Ibid.

The major news media—particularly television—focused on disruptions and damage caused by the protests, triggering anti-demonstration demonstrations, many apparently instigated by government operatives.[151] Independent transmission of news virtually ceased to exist after Vicente Fox's "by entrepreneurs for entrepreneurs" government granted duopoly rights to the country's two communications giants, Televisa and TV Azteca, in 2005. Local newspapers continued to publish, most of them thanks to government advertising, but even those that maintained full editorial and reporting staffs increased dependence upon international wire services like Reuters and the Associated Press.[152]

Although the wire services boasted "instant coverage," as they increased their technological capacities, they simultaneously reduced their reporting staffs. In 2007, Dan Feder in the online *Narco News Bulletin* described wire service journalists as "desk correspondents gleaning

---

150 Marc Lacey, "Human Rights Defenders Seek Protection in Mexico," *New York Times,* June 19, 2010.

151 That disruptions of work and family life—and damage to property and financial well-being—existed, shouldn't be overlooked. No matter how justified mass protests might have seemed to the participants, "they played hell with those of us struggling to keep our jobs and support our families," a single mother from Rosario, near Mazatlán, Sinaloa, told me. Demonstrations triggered massive traffic backups, overheated cars, bawling children, calls to the police. Schools and businesses closed and construction projects encountered delays and vandalism. Employers docked the pay of workers arriving late; others slept in their cars overnight because conflicts made commutes impossible. Fights broke out between demonstrators and those opposed to them, usually with injuries, occasionally with loss of lives. Providers cancelled deliveries of propane, water, and other necessities, and garbage piled up in areas involved.

152 Both the daily *La Jornada* and the weekly magazine *Proceso* had national Distribution, but national television was confined to Televisa and TV Azteca. The two television giants also controlled most of the AM and FM stations. They were among the wealthiest corporations in the nation and had strong ties to the conservative government of President Felipe Calderón—ties so strong that it often was suggested that they ran the government, and the president and Congress served their interests rather than the reverse.

stories from local newspapers and taking phone calls."[153] Carlos Payán, the founding editor of the daily *La Jornada*, told a "Mexico's Situation" forum in Saltillo, Mexico, in 2009 that the Mexican media had ceased to be operated by journalists and had passed into the hands of entrepreneurs who "deform and erode information and any attempts at objectivity."[154]

Federal incursions into the mountainous areas of southern Mexico demolished the facilities of community radio stations, many of which broadcast in *indigena* languages. Officials cited technical or licensing violations, but the broadcasters and their audiences assured human rights advocates that the punitive actions, which included the assassinations of two young Trique broadcasters in Oaxaca, were launched because the stations were providing news and commentary in *indigena* languages and disregarding governmental versions of regional events.

The television duopoly, most major AM radio stations, and national newspapers often omitted news critical of the government, including military killings of civilians, even when their reporters had covered those events.[155] Government propaganda about the "well-being" of the nation, morally and financially, and its urgings to repress "negativism" and criticism of official policies further alienated Mexico's citizenry from the country's small coterie of power wielders as the value of the peso declined and layoffs increased.[156]

---

153 Dan Feder, *Narco News Bulletin* (date not available).

154 Leopoldo Ramos, "Protagonizaría la clase media el próximo estallido social," *La Jornada*, November 29, 2009.

155 During a forum on torture as a repressive tool, University of the City of Mexico professor Clemencia Correa asked participants how many had heard or read about drug corporation beheadings, then about the treatment of political prisoners jailed after the militarized Atenco assault. The response to the first question was a unanimous yes, the response to the second prompted only two attendees to raise their hands.

156 The Banco de Mexico countered the falling value of the peso on the international exchange rate by pumping money from its reserves into the hands of speculators, thus depriving the citizenry of desperately needed funds for employment, food, clothing, housing, transportation, and education.

By 2006, the PAN administration, the television giants, and the hierarchy of the Catholic Church had effectively joined forces to restrict citizen participation in political and social decision-making, paving the way for neo-liberal entrepreneurs to accumulate immense wealth and the Church to actively promote legislation concerning social protest and abortion rights. For seventy years the single-party PRI government had demanded acceptance and compliance. Questioning authority or doctrine or questioning traditional patterns of male superiority, family obedience and social conformity fostered independent thought and action, and independent thought and action threatened the status quo and those profiting from it. Protest demonstrations and movements were described as "Communist-inspired" or "leftist-led," and the members branded as "dissidents" and "revolutionaries."

"In the media dissidence is attacked, and in the atmosphere of false religiosity the existence of true dialogue is not just a 'rupture of institutional order' but a heresy," Carlos Monsiváis insisted in *Tiempo de Saber.*[157] José Joaquín Blanco concluded, "It makes it difficult to argue for freedom of expression for the minority if it's denied to the majority."[158]

"It is as though a hundred million people are crouched in the shadows watching a fictional television show called 'our government,'" retired business owner Luis de la Vega told me as we chatted on the patio of his hillside home north of Guanajuato in central Mexico. "Like a *lucha libre* (pro wrestling) performance, bright lights and grunts and waving to the crowd, it's all fake, everybody knows it's fake. Our leaders have beautiful wives, they have mansions and big cars and herds of bodyguards and they tell us how good things are and we have less and less. But we're just audience, hypnotized ..."

Clearing his throat and forcing himself upright, he insisted, "Religion is the opiate of the people. No, the media is."

---

157 Julio Scherer-García and Carlos Monsiváis, *Tiempo de saber* (2003).
158 José Joaquín Blanco, *Un chavo bien helado* (1990).

111

The student uprising of 1968, although violently repressed by the police and military, shook the foundations of the tightly structured PRI government. Educated and ambitious young students were not the obedient sons and daughters that the system required, nor did they view presidents and governors as godly personages whose actions, personally and politically, could not be questioned, challenged, or opposed. Products of an educational system that included the country's largest and most prestigious university, they sought heroes outside the cant of PRI-regulated primary and secondary school textbooks. They learned to read and speak other languages, particularly English, and absorbed American and European values from television, advertising, and the increasing numbers of Mexican nationals who had traveled in and lived in other countries.

Before neo-liberal Miguel de la Madrid (1982-1988) assumed the presidency, many of the country's diplomats had been representatives of Mexican culture—writers (even poets), artists, intellectuals. But as higher education and the humanities became politically suspect, the neo-liberal presidents named loyal operatives to the majority of diplomatic posts. They also filled most of the important cabinet positions with political operatives who had little or no experience in the areas they were assigned to manage. Their decisions, often dictated by those who had appointed them, triggered conflicts, particularly with *campesino* and labor organizations as technocracy supplanted education and the majority of the country's most able and provocative thinkers were excluded from the governing process.

The financial collapse of the 1980s, triggered in large part by the billions of dollars of debt accrued in the modernization of the petroleum industry, the annual migration of hundreds of thousands of Mexican workers to the United States and the increasing participation of transnational corporations in the country's economic life, distorted the traditional "our father the state" and "our father the church" structure. The escalating market for narcotics in the United States pulled billions of dollars through Mexico, creating opportunities for enrichment based on enterprise and daring rather than inheritance and social status. Increased participation by women in the country's social and financial life eroded conformance to male dominated households. Church membership plummeted during the last three decades of the twentieth century as social roles changed, migration split families, and the traditional male-breadwinner/woman *ama-de-casa* family gave way to urban needs for multiple incomes, commuting, and diverse educational and environmental challenges.

Neither the Church hierarchy nor the PRI seemed able to move with these changes. Both insisted on the observance of outmoded values even when their individual actions and policies sidestepped them. The concept of "we Mexicans" (that incorporated "we Mexicans who believe in the Catholic Church") gave way to a more personal "I José" or "I María" individualism, particularly among young people.

Young Mexicans growing up in urban or suburban environments perceived the hypocrisy that existed between their parents' and grandparents' morality and the society that engulfed them, but the majority of them had no viable new systems to insert in the old ones' place. Combined with increased mobility among the population, which included the rural-to-urban movement of millions of *campesinos* and small landholders and the magnet provided by work opportunities in the United States, the nation's young became increasingly less willing to accept lack of opportunity, poverty, and oppression. The social pact that had existed for centuries between the minority that governed and the majority that were governed began to shred, paving the way for challenges to government authority.

Participants in a "What Happened to Democracy?" forum in Mexico City in 2007 elaborated changes that had occurred after the conservative PAN government rose to presidential power in 2000. Among their observances was the increased power that PRI governors and local caciques had gained. No longer under disciplined top-to-bottom federal control, governors like Ulisés Ruiz in Oaxaca became PRI kingpins, accruing enormous wealth in the

113

process.[159] At the same time, the wobbly PAN federal administration had to prop itself on borrowed shoulders— support by segments of the PRI, PRD, and other political parties and monopolized entrepreneurs like TV Azteca's Ricardo Salinas and Televisa's Emilio Ascárraga. As a result, these entrepreneurs and corporations controlled many aspects of the government instead of the government controlling them.

"We don't know who's calling the shots," one of the What Happened to Democracy? participants complained. "Is the government taking orders from Televisa? The capos? The United States?" Many of those attending concluded that whoever was giving the orders cared only for their own wealth and were willing to see the country deteriorate.

"For the Spanish crown of the sixteenth century," Subcomandante Insurgente Marcos insists in Oaxaca, the First Stele, "like the neoliberalism of the beginning of the twenty-first century, the only culture is the one they dominate. Indigenous lands were nothing but an abundant source of labor for the Spanish powers, as they are now for savage capitalism."[160]

Despite so-called reforms, constitutional guarantees, and supposed concessions on the part of the federal government, the majority of Mexico's indigena population achieved very few gains under Mexico's federal government and "remain unheard and unattended," journalist Juan Pablo Montes-Jiménez quoted labor leader Raúl Hilario Sánchez during the latter's appearance in Oaxaca's poverty-wracked Mixteca in 2009.[161]

"The conditions of poverty and margination of the pueblos is the road for an upcoming social revolution, and the government of Mexico alone is responsible," Sánchez insisted. The marginally employed, the unemployed, and

---

159 Ruiz caustically replied to efforts to depose him in 2006, "Only God can remove a governor!"

160 Subcomandante Insurgente Marcos, The Speed of Dreams, ed. Canek Peña-Vargas and Greg Ruggiero (2007).

161 Juan Pablo Montes Jimènez, "La pobreza puede propiciar surgimiento de grupos armados," Noticias Voz e imagen de Oaxaca," April 22, 2009.

hundreds of thousands of debtors besieged by bills they couldn't pay echoed that belief. Every month during 2008-2010 more and more beggars appeared on city streets. Every hike in the cost of public services—domestic gas, electricity, transportation—prompted residents to do without, triggering more price hikes, because the government needed operating funds.

The government was operating—but primarily for the benefit of its officeholders. The worst months of the economic crisis (October 2008-May 2009) thrust nearly 750,000 workers out of their jobs as inflation increased and federal and local governments reduced services. Mayors and municipal presidents abandoned construction projects and laid off employees, including police and firemen. The drastic reduction in money being sent by emigrants working in the United States further impoverished already struggling marginal communities.[162]

"The fatal bullet," a retired aluminum plant foreman described the 2008-2009 crisis during a conversation I had with him. "It killed what already was a quivering corpse."

In 2010, President Calderón complained about "low consumer confidence" without mentioning that the lack of disposal income had created the diminished buying power he was attempting to encourage. Months earlier, trying to explain the escalation of the prices of domestic gas, water, and fuel, he told the Mexican people, "If we arrive at a point where poor families consume less water without sacrificing their well-being and consume less electricity, we are going to help those families save money and save our own budget, because each kilowatt that is not consumed represents a subsidy that we don't have to pay."[163]

By 2010, street crime and violence had become so commonplace "we shrug it off, it's like floods, droughts,

---

162 Mexican Association of Municipalities, 2009. The Association reported that 95 percent of the country's municipalities (equivalent to U.S. counties) were bankrupt.

163 Todd Miller, "Is a Social Explosion in the Wings?" *NACLA Report on the Americas,* September 29, 2009. Calderón made no mention of having rich families or transnational corporations make the same sacrifices.

earthquakes, a natural event," retired professor David Castro e-mailed me from Zacatecas where he lived.

Natural? Those most assiduously protesting government policies insisted that life in Mexico was so *un*natural it had become surreal. Demonstrators in Mexico City denounced Calderón's economic policies after the federal government cancelled the May 1 May Day celebration (equivalent to the U.S.'s Labor Day), insisting that the president "correct his social and economic policies that were thrusting the country into backwardness."[164] They further insisted that "dialogue with the government is worn out and broken." Although demonstrations were necessary to show authorities how the public felt they could not sufficiently curb the government from imposing whatever reforms it chose.

Lázaro García, national leader and spokesperson of the Frente Revolucionario Popular (FPR), told *El Milenio*'s Diego Enrique Osorno that the country was not yet ripe for a full scale social movement that would affect dramatic governmental changes. García explained that Mexico's increasingly fascist government was finding it more and more necessary to use a military presence to enforce its doctrines, but the masses hadn't yet reached sufficient awareness of their potential strength to unite and create a new national government.

"They [the federal government] have the military—but it's not a totally indoctrinated military." Its hold, García insisted, was tenuous and vulnerable, but the masses needed to organize in order to nullify its power.[165]

The Popular Assembly of Oaxaca and most other protesting organizers and organizations in Mexico insisted that movements for change—protests, work stoppages, demonstrations—had to be accomplished without violence. Federal and state governments imposed no such restrictions on their security forces. Cities throughout the country were being torn apart by gunfire, military takeovers, slayings, and beheadings, most of which

---

164 Patricia Muñoz-Rios, "Fourteen thousand march to urge changes in economic policy," *La Jornada,* June 4, 2009.
165 Diego Osorno, *Oaxaca sitiada* (2007).

government authorities attributed to gang members and organized crime.

Governing authorities enclosed in "PAN-landia," a make-believe country of happy people enthralled with bicentennial celebrations and the national soccer team, shunted aside protest as "a tiny minority" stirring up desperation and disobedience.

"In Oaxaca, it's a crime to write! It's a crime to protest! It's a crime to think!" newspaper correspondent Pedro Matias told members of a Rights Action human rights delegation. Protesting farmers in San Luis Potosí battered their state governor with eggs, because he failed to acknowledge their complaints about inflation and unemployment. The wives of miners buried by a cave-in at Pasta de Conchos in northern Mexico blocked access to the site of the tragedy shouting, "The government wants to forget what happened! Pretend we don't exist!"

The parents of nearly a hundred victims of a fire that destroyed a privatized government infant care facility in Chihuahua pounded on bureaucrats' doors demanding, "Why are you ignoring us?" "We want to be heard!" came from human rights advocates whose documented reports of violations were shelved, journalists whose coworkers had been beaten or killed, *indigena* communities whose homes were raided and burned by government-equipped paramilitaries, churchmen who saw drug dealers openly recruit adherents in their communities, writers who reported the private enrichment of high-ranking government officials and had defamation charges filed against them.[166]

"We have no place to turn, no one to turn to," I heard over and over. Both the government of Mexico and that of the United States continued to promote the War on Drugs at the expense of hundreds of thousands of citizens, whose complaints went unanswered.[167] Auto-sufficient farming

---

166 For a more detailed account see Robert Joe Stout, Robert "We Want To Be Heard," *New Politics,* Winter 2011.

167 Human Rights Watch, *Uniform Impunity,* April 29, 2009. The document reported that Mexico's National Human Rights Commission received 3,399 complaints against the military from 2007 to the end of 2009, including allegations of rapes,

disappeared as men deserted their crops, both out of fear and to take work constructing roads for drug smugglers and illegal lumbering operations.[168] Competing drug organizations commandeered entire towns, instigating Hatfield-McCoy type feuds that took hundreds of lives. In those areas, the only government that existed was that imposed by the *capos* and timber companies.

For the exploited, those *"desde abajo"* ("from down beneath," a term used by both the Zapatistas and Oaxaca's Popular Assembly to describe persons disconnected from the ruling elite), the gap between their lives and their needs and the operations of the two governments was exacerbated by the freedom with which entrepreneurs and the monied class controlled the flow of labor, goods, and wealth. Other than being able to vote (although not to select the candidates for whom they can cast ballots) they and the organizations that represented them—NGOs, labor unions, human rights and environmental groups, and university researchers and writers—lacked effective input into the decisions being made by the two nations' rulers and by entrepreneurial associations like the Security and Prosperity Partnership (SSP) and the North American Competitive Council (NACC).[169]

Heavily armed security forces restricted access to the SSP summit meetings, much as they have done to other international collaborations of heads of state, like the World Trade Organization. Most of the details of the so-called "Plan Mérida," which provided armaments and

homicides, arbitrary detentions, and tortures. During this time few complaints were investigated by military authorities and only three convictions were recorded.

168 Kent Paterson, "Mexico's New Dirty War," http://americas.ircnline.org/am/6714, 2010.

169 The SSP is a three-nation consortium (the United States, Canada, and Mexico) of governmental and private executives whose negotiations and decisions are not open to the public. It was formed as "NAFTA-Plus" in 2005. The NACC emerged the following year to enable governments to recognize the importance of business issues to the overall social welfare and to free transnational (i.e. U.S. and Canadian) corporations to do what they wanted without interference from the legislative branches of the three countries.

training to Mexican security forces, emerged from SSP meetings before they were presented to the congresses of the two countries for modifications and approval. Federal police and the military were the primary anti-protest forces used to repress the citizen uprisings at Atenco and in Oaxaca. They and government-equipped paramilitaries restricted Zapatista expansion in Chiapas. Soldiers forcibly evicted union workers during the takeovers of the Luz y Fuerza del Centro and crushed the Grupo Mexico strikes in Cananea and Pasto de Conchos. Those actions intensified the frustrations of those who were protesting economic and environmental conditions—protests the government passed over or refused to acknowledge. A *Witness for Peace* bulletin warned,

> If the "Plan Mexico" proposal is any indication, the SPP is going well beyond the economic realm. Taking into account the wealth disparity, extreme poverty, and levels of migration exacerbated by policies such as NAFTA, many wonder if the next key ingredient to any trade agreement would be security measures to both quell the inevitable social discontent and protect private investment.

Criminalizing popular protests and repressing them by force, like criminalizing undocumented entry by immigrants fleeing from poverty and militarizing a war against narcotic dealers fulfilling an undiminished existent market, has not only cost the two countries billions of dollars that could have been used to legitimately employ, feed, and clothe their citizenry, but has driven those in authority to increasingly stricter methods of control. By 2010, the governments of the two countries had made a farce of the "aren't we happy, proud and obedient" *telenovela* prosperity they'd tried to display. Like parents who become increasingly punitive with children they term disrespectful and disobedient and wind up engendering hatred and criminal responses, the governments of Mexico and the United States had created monsters that by 2010 they no longer could completely control.

For the protagonists of the *telenovela*, a happy ending was doubtful.

SECTION IV - CORRUPTION

1

"Despite what the president says, this *pinche país* ranks last in Latin America—maybe in the world—in being able to compete industrially, in spending on social services and education, in having a plan to move ahead. We're dead in the water and he tells us how good things are. *Caca!* What have we got? The world's richest man and 100 million *pobres,* that's what!"

Julia Alarcón made no pretense when I talked to her in Mexico City in 2009 that she was a political expert.

"I'm a psychologist. That means I talk to a lot of people, see a lot of things. I know the country is in bad shape. Worse, from most indications, than in 1910."

She admitted that most of what she knew she'd acquired from sources other than government influenced—conversations, online analyses, books—which led her to believe that the federal government was trying to conceal that it had become a rudderless ship heaved this way and that by forces it couldn't control: powerful drug corporations, foreign investors, the television duopoly, the Catholic Church. And by the corruption that had eaten away its internal processes.

Alarcón's observations, shared by many in Mexico, coincide with Gaetano Mosca's definition of governments: Whether monarchial, oligarchy, or democratic, political systems consist of a ruling political minority dominating the majority by being organized, dynamic, and clear about its objectives. Whether this elite was created through inheritance, through wealth, or by ambition, personality, and capacity for work, it incorporated traditions of the culture to which it belonged, thus, the governmental framework varied from one civilization to another. But a consistent factor in all societies, from the least developed to those with the most extensive technology and power, was political and social control of the governed by those who wielded power and reaped the most benefits from it.[170]

Political changes occurred when the existent elite was overthrown or pushed aside by forces more dynamic and organized than it had become. In twenty-first century Mexico, the wealthy drug corporations, the entrepreneurial class, U.S.-dominated neoliberal economics, and the Church challenged the political control that was slipping out of the federal government's grasp. As these forces competed, using whatever means necessary to gain greater power or concentrate it in the hands of a new elite, the existent government became a force in name only, represented by actors parading as legislators and department heads who entertained the public but no longer served it.

Political changes do not necessarily mean changes in governmental structure. Many voters, including liberals who bolted the PRD to support Vicente Fox's presidential bid in 2000, anticipated that Fox would engineer a populist, business-oriented government by taking it out of the hands of the *"perfumados"* of the PRI neo-liberal years.[171] A majority of voters (and those who didn't vote) suspected that he would do no more than move the government towards a more balanced left-right orientation, not institute structural changes. ("A little bit different but more of the same.")

Despite the "man of the people" bravado of his electoral campaign, which included touting his connections with his "amigou" George Bush, Fox wilted under criticism and ceded much of his constitutional power to the entrepreneurial elite. In similar fashion, his successor, Felipe Calderón, became primarily a PAN publicist, buoyed by a subservient cabinet composed predominantly of conservative Catholic appointees, many of whom lacked

---

170 Gaetano Mosca, "Glosario de Conceptos Políticos Usuales," Uemed.net *Enciclopedia Virtual*

171 *"Perfumados"* was a journalistic term given to Carlos Salinas de Gortari and his cabinet officials, many of whom had been educated in the United States, dressed elegantly, and spent lavishly.

backgrounds in the areas they were appointed to supervise.

The revolution that began in 1910 and elevated Madero to the presidency a year later did not revoke the old elitist system nor create something totally new. Madero was assassinated after a year in office, purportedly by followers of revolutionary general Huerta; armed conflict between opposing groups lasted for another fifteen years. The new "democracy" installed nearly two decades after the revolution began did not differ greatly from the Porfirio Díaz dictatorship of 1870 to 1910. The elite retained their commercial and political power and the presidents after Lázaro Cárdenas, each appointed by his predecessor, reinforced the PRI's vertical structure and dominant executive branch.[172]

By 2009, nearly half of the federal budget was devoted to paying salaries and benefits to the country's bulging bureaucracy. Legislators ranked among the highest salaried non-executives in the country.[173]

"They think to govern is synonymous with to entertain ... it's not important to them that they spend public money

---

172 Before the year 2000 elections, the PRI did away with the *"dedazo"* and staged primary elections.

173 The *Diario Oficial de la Federación* listed a federal deputy's base salary at Mex\$105,370 per month plus an additional Mex\$45,786 for attending legislative sessions, i.e. Mex\$152,000 per month, plus bonuses including a retirement plan in which the deputy could deposit 12 percent of his earnings and the government would match that amount, over Mex\$28,000 for *"ayuda ciudadana"* (essentially aid to his or her constituency), free medical and dental care for the deputy, his parents, and his family, airline tickets, travel mileage, year-end bonuses equal to a month's salary, vacations, cell phones, cars and drivers, and office staff. Supreme Court justices received slightly less than Mex\$350,000 a month, plus bi-weekly bonuses, vacation bonuses (50 percent of ten days of their salary for each vacation period), a Christmas bonus of forty-days salary, two vehicles at their disposal, free cell phone and wireless internet use, a food budget, life insurance, retirement pension, and health insurance. The minimum wage in Mexico's Federal District, by contrast, was Mex\$54 per day. In 2010, President Calderón justified the amounts paid to the justices and election officials by asserting "they provide much more value than that through the work they do."

to cosmeticize their photo-shop appearance and their political activities with infomercials," journalist Jenero Villamil described "the new generation of politicians" in a 2009 syndicated article.[174] Absenteeism for legislative sessions and committee meetings forced postponements and cancellations. Frequently, legislators voted for bills they hadn't read and evaded taking stands on critical issues like those involving drug-related organized crime.

By 2010, over two-thirds of the population earned too little to provide basic necessities while those in power lavished millions on extravagant travel expenses and expanded state and federal security forces. Several governors earned more than the presidents of many European countries, the infant mortality rate in rural areas rose to almost 50 percent, deaths from preventable diseases soared, and hospitals and clinics closed for the lack of staff and medicines. Legislators, cabinet secretaries, governors, and municipal presidents functioned more like actors in badly staged and poorly directed theatrical comedies than they did as lawmakers. Some like Estado de Mexico governor Peña Nieto popped up in *telenovelas*—as themselves, receiving praise wrenched into the scripts to boost their presidential or gubernatorial candidacies.

"More than votes they want fans," Villamil commented.

2

The failures of PRI candidates Labastida in 2000 and Madrazo in 2006 to garner enough votes to enable the PRI to repeat the fraud of 1988 altered the nation's way of practicing politics. Television played an increasingly dominant role: Viewers throughout the nation saw what the candidates looked like, what charisma they exuded and whether or not they appeared to be trustworthy and strong enough to fit a pre-conceived presidential image. Vicente Fox's 2000 vernacular "nonpolitician" stance stimulated thousands of PRI and PRD adherents to vote for him and for changes that never occurred. The PRI's return to

---

174 Jenaro Villamil, "La nueva generación de políticos," *Noticias, Voz e Imagen de Oaxaca,* September 2009.

dominance during the mid-term 2009 elections prompted the opposing political parties to form awkward coalitions between the right-wing PRI and the liberal PRD that won the governorship of three states the following year.[175]

"The political parties' battle for power has nothing to do with principles or ideology," insisted Octavio Rodriguez-Araujo. "What is most important are the individuals and their backgrounds, cosmetized or real, not the principles that the parties claim to possess."[176] The coalitions offered no solid agendas, no consistent governing plans, no pragmatic (or even theoretical) economic policies. By having become popularity contests, they induced those striving for control to boost telegenic figureheads who would conform to their wishes. Fox's "government of, by and for entrepreneurs" supplanted the country's political leaders with teleprompter readers extolling their patrons' products.

Like many others in Mexico, Julia Alarcón insisted that Calderón's 2006 election was immersed in fraud. PAN's control of the television duopoly (or the duopoly's control of Calderón) and propaganda bombardments elevating the War on Drugs to a crusade of good against evil enabled him to maintain his fragile hold on a legislative branch's squabbling over apportionments and tax increases.

Although Calderón in June 2007 declared that as president he served "the state" in which the only legitimate power resided, not in individuals or political parties. And immediately after he took office, he began tightening links to the military, much as nineteenth and twentieth century presidents throughout Latin America had done. Minority rights campaigner Antonio Bolaños scoffed at Calderón's "pious" assertion about service as he tugged a group of newspaper photos from a thick manila folder and placed them in front of me.

A *Milenio* photo showed Calderón in military garb in December 2006 accompanied by General Guillermo

---

175 Although it should be noted that two of the three were lifelong *priistas* who'd been passed over as candidates by their state organizations.

176 Octavio Rodríguez-Araujo, articulos, http://rodriguezaraujo.unam.mx.

Galván, his recently named secretary of defense. One from *Proceso* showed him flanked by Galván and Secretary of the Navy Admiral Saynez smiling for cameramen. Others showed him declaring immunity for the military, campaigning for constitutional changes that would grant sweeping powers to the armed forces, and posing with Galván and Saynez as he announced the deployment of thousands of troops to areas bordering the United States.

"He wants to be another Porfirio Díaz, but he can't pull it off," Bolaños grunted. "He's nothing but a damned puppet master so focused on playing with his toys that he hasn't noticed that he has no audience anymore."

Galván, Saynez, and the series of secretaries of the government were some of these toys, each of them singing the company song as they accumulated wealth for their performances. A "get-what-you-can-while-you-can" attitude permeated the nation. It was the motivation for the drug corporations' takeovers of territory and businesses and the motivation for quick profits by entrepreneurs and politicians who exhibited a "to-hell-with-the-future" disregard for ethics, poverty, and ecological devastation.

Despite increasing reliance on the military to combat drug cultivation and exportation and to repress unionism and popular protest, by 2010 Calderón's government had become a hollow shell. He filled cabinet posts with inexperienced subalterns who endorsed his rigidly Catholic pro-privatization philosophy but were no match for experienced entrepreneurs and the dominating criminal *capos* who had undermined many government functions, particularly those of the police and the military.

By 2010, over 50,000 Mexican citizens had lost their lives in the drug corporations' battles with each other and with the military and law enforcement. Tepid negotiations to achieve greater U.S. support in controlling military-type arms exports brought promises but no substantial results.

Human rights representatives in the northern states of Baja California and Chihuahua refused to process abuses by Mexico's military (including theft, wrongful arrest, rape, and torture), because residents who had filed complaints had been waylaid and beaten by unidentified government supporters. In the southern state of Oaxaca, over 100 murders remained unsolved in 2006, but federal and state police and soldiers arrested and tortured over 140 peaceful demonstrators and a local judge sentenced them to federal prison for "sedition." Only Mexican politicians ranked lower on national polls about respect and trust than the police.

Despite countless promises to purge all levels of law enforcement of its criminal and drug corporation-associated elements, the majority of changes were cosmetic. Journalists and academic specialists in security and law enforcement questioned Calderón's insistence on promoting legislation to substitute a single federal police force for municipal and state law enforcement agencies. (Various members of Congress and several governors also disapproved of the proposal.)

Syndicated cartoonist Rafael Barajas—"El Fisgón"—told a Feria del Libro audience in Oaxaca in 2010 that he believed Calderón was setting up a situation where it would be necessary to declare *"an estado de excepción"* that would lead to a militarized takeover and cancellation of the 2012 presidential elections. Narco News journalist Kristin Bricker cited reports by Mexico's secret service agency, CISEN, that the "drug cartels' control likely extends from local police forces and legislatures up to the federal Congress."[177]

Federalizing police forces under one command, as Calderón proposed, wouldn't have altered the "Amway System" under which most law enforcement agencies operated.[178] *Plazas* (positions within the force, such as motorcycle patrol, vice investigation, etc.) were purchased by one seeking advancement and the purchaser paid a weekly or monthly quota to the higher-up from whom he acquired his new position. That higher-up in turn paid his superior, since he too acquired his position after serving an even higher higher-up. As officials were promoted, they took their *hijos* ("children") with them, thus perpetrating

---

177 Kristin Bricker, mywordismyweapon.blogsport.com.
178 Information taken from interviews with former police and police commanders in Baja California, the Federal District, and the Estado de Mexico, 1993-1995 and 2007-2008. See José Luis Trueba Lara, *Los Primeros en Morir,* Nueva Imagen, Mexico (1996) for an excellent description of how this system was practiced.

the flow of money collection in much the same way that Amway and similar businesses conducted sales.

Often the amounts of the quotas of those on the lower levels of the pyramid exceeded the salaries the police were being paid, making it imperative that they extort money through bribes, theft, concealing the activities of criminals, and protection services. The *hijo's patrón* abandoned him if he failed to meet his quotas, and he was given *la baja* (fired) or assigned to bank guard or watchman duties where he had little chance of collecting bribes; consequently, he spent much of his on-duty time extorting payments from motorists, businesses, pickpockets, prostitutes, and whoever else he could shake down.

Elected federal officials and many holding major state offices reported criminal cases "resolved" that had merely been archived but never investigated. A former federal administrative employee told me that this often was done to inflate statistics that had dipped to an alarming conviction rate of 4 percent of those charged with crimes in 2008. A former federal investigator admitted in conversations I had with him that police commonly relied on victims and informants to locate offenders and wrested confessions by beating those accused, giving them electrical shocks and threatening to rape or kill their wives and children.

"They put on uniforms to collect bribes and direct traffic, but they are just another of the criminal bands that prey on Mexico's citizenry," a retired Mexican chemical engineer wrote on Facebook. Although more than 1,000 *feminicidos* remain uninvestigated and unresolved, the police arrested and Mexican courts sentenced over thirty young women to up to thirty years imprisonment for having abortions. (More than 140 others were being processed for the same charges in 2009.)[179]

---

179 *Feminicidios* in Spanish defines the killing of women because of gender. In 2010, public protests in Guanajuato and Jalisco prompted the release of some of the women charged and the reduction of some sentences to eight instead of thirty years. None of those who had been imprisoned had been charged with "abortion" or "illegal abortion" but with murder (infanticide).

Throughout the first four years of Calderón's term as president of Mexico (2006-2010), security—and the lack of it as the drug corporations became increasingly powerful—surmounted all other issues in most Mexicans' consideration. Support of the militarization of the War on Drugs wavered, but a large proportion of the country's populace, like the politicians supposedly leading them, saw no other solution than to fight force with force. Federal officials tried to minimize the drug corporations' takeovers of land, municipal and state governments and business transactions, citing "security reasons" for withholding information about financial dealings and their own power grabs.

When the federal legislature demanded the documentation used to justify the government's October 2009 takeover of the Luz y Fuerza del Centro (LFC) and the elimination of the electrician's union, officials responded bluntly that the documents were classified for "reasons of national security."[180] Deputy Mario di Costanzo accused Hacienda Sub-Secretary Dionisio Pérez-Jácome of falsifying the data provided to the Supreme Court before it rendered judgment on the union's application for a stay in the governmental action and lying to the Legislature when he explained the "legality" of the takeover.[181]

The Supreme Court verdict—like all verdicts rendered by Mexico's judicial system—did not determine innocence or guilt on any party's part. Courts evaluated only the paperwork (or more recently in some states the oral testimony in criminal cases) to determine the legality of the charges and counter charges. In the LFC, the court ruled that the government's action was valid, but the justices did not, di Costanzo insisted, avail themselves of information they should have had, because the government had withheld it.

Calderón and Secretary of Labor Lozano boasted about creating jobs but failed to acknowledge that the majority of

---

180 Occupation of the company's facilities by the military and federal police and the abolishment of the electrical workers union was done by presidential order.

181 Andrea Becerril, "Irresponsable, el aval de la Corte sobre LFC," *La Jornada,* July 11, 2010.

new jobs created during 2009-2010 were temporary, low paying, and most were replacements for salaried permanent employees who'd been terminated.[182] In January 2009, INEGI (National Institute of Statistics and Geography) reported that 900 persons a day were losing their employment, largely because exports had declined to two-thirds of their 2007 level, and inflation had risen nearly 10 percent on basic consumer items.[183] The administration tried to counter discontent with assurances of the solvency of the Mexican economy and comparisons with other countries whose exports and currency had suffered even worse declines.

Federal officials contended that by continuing to bolster the pesos' status against international currencies, they could control internal inflation and as a result minimize price increases. Theoretically, this maneuver would give citizens more ability to purchase the goods and services they needed. Calderón publicly insisted that greater "consumer confidence" was necessary and would generate more income and, consequently, more employment but sidestepped considerations that "it's not consumer confidence it's consumer money that's lacking," as an airline pilot who had to take a huge salary reduction in order to stay employed complained.

Julio Boltvinik, of the Colegio de México, scored Calderón for lamenting that Carlos Slim and other entrepreneurs profiting during the financial crisis of 2007-2009 were not paying taxes but "the only thing he did was cry like any ordinary citizen, demonstrating the impotence of this government, of an executive branch that before was strong."[184]

182 Patricia Muñoz-Ríos, "Manipuladas, cifras sobre desempleo," *La Jornada*, September 6, 2010. In the same issue Carlos Fernández-Vega amply details the gains and losses among both permanent and temporary employees and salary differences involved including the decline of workers enrolled in Seguro Social.

183 Mexico News & Analysis, January 5-25, reported 400,000 lost jobs during the last two months of 2008, an even greater employment decrease.

184 Susana Gonzàlez G., "Aclaraciones a la miscelánea fiscal reducirán el ISR a grandes

Although Article 31 of Mexico's constitution stipulated that taxation be equitable and in proportion for all citizens, the country's 400-plus major entrepreneurs paid only 1.8 percent of their earnings in federal ISR taxes (*impuesto sobre la renta*—the equivalent of U.S. income tax); small business and individual wage and salary earners paid 28 percent.[185] Tax legislation passed in 1973 allowed corporations to consolidate their incomes and tax debts with tributaries that reported huge losses and/or expenses, which significantly reduced their obligations. After 1994, the federal government failed to aggressively pursue non-payment by mayor corporations, a number of which slid years behind in remitting even reduced obligations.

Calderón's non-leadership combined with privatization policies, many at the instigation of the International Monetary Fund, opened the door for investment schemes that enriched the few at the expense of the many. One of the most notorious consisted of reforming the government employees' retirement and health system by moving the funds they were accumulating into the hands of private investors whose remuneration was based on the volume they handled, not how the funds performed. The financial crash of 2008 wiped out years of workers' savings, but the investors continued to profit even when they made risky or faulty distributions. Financial columnist Arturo Alcalde-Justiano accused Calderon of "deceiving the workers by promising them better pensions when in fact the private investors were the principal benefactors" of the new law.[186]

Boltvinik labeled Calderón's economic policies a manipulation to create millions of poor citizens and to support monopolies that would ensure entrepreneurial wealth. In 1993, Carlos Salinas de Gortari confronted the country's financial crisis and tumbling peso-to-the-dollar

empresas," *La Jornada,* March 12, 2010.

185 Some major participants in the Mexican stock exchange paid no taxes. Cementos Mexicanos, for example, reported income of Mex$243 billion in 2008, paid zero taxes, and received a federal tax credit of over 440 million.

186 *La Jornada,* September 1, 2007. It should be noted that the reform involving retirement funds was supported by the Senate and House of Deputies by an overwhelming margin.

rate by assembling twenty-nine of Mexico's wealthiest and most successful magnates and asserting that those assembled, being highly successful and convincing entrepreneurs, had the ability to raise Mex$75 million each to resolve the country's overwhelming debt. The magnates responded positively; in fact, Emilio Azcárraga, the owner of Televisa, averred that he could come up with more than the suggested Mex$75 million.[187]

This bailout—business to the government rather than the reverse—carried a long-term price tag. Televisa became a controlling political power, as did other major contributors: enormous tax breaks, the granting of monopoly powers, lessening environmental restrictions, permitting company controlled unions to replace independents. PAN and PRI candidates (including Felipe Calderón during his 2006 presidential campaign) courted these entrepreneurs and obligingly repaid them once the candidates were elected.

Government collaboration with the television duopoly and financial control of much of the print media transcended laws limiting and/or prohibiting government officials from profiting financially from activities they were supposed to regulate.[188] Despite the deteriorating financial situation that was driving millions of workers below the poverty level, the federal government excused billions of dollars in corporation taxes owed by the major corporations and failed to pursue investigations of other billions that Pemex and other government agencies could not account for. Meanwhile, high-ranking federal officials, including the late Juan Camilo Mouriño and Genero García-Luna, accumulated wealth that far exceeded what they were earning from their salaries.

The amounts that they accumulated didn't equal what entrepreneur Carlos Slim was hauling in. Calculated at

---

187 Jorge Zepeda-Patterson, *Los amos de Mexico* (2007).

188 Both print and electronic media depended heavily on government advertising, and although newspapers and TV and radio commentators reported complaints or denouncements by civic and political groups, they did not (with a few exceptions, notably the daily *La Jornada* and weekly *Proceso*) take strong editorial stances or campaign against the reported abuses.

various times by *Forbes* to be the richest man in the world, Slim manipulated PAN's "government of, by and for" entrepreneurial system to his advantage. His wealth and control of a major portion of the country's communications systems through Telmex gave him a privileged position vis-à-vis government regulators.

"He tells them what to do," a business competitor complained, "not the reverse."[189]

The television duopoly of Televisa and TV Aztec and their radio outlets regularly omitted reportage of incidents or issues unfavorable to the government.[190] Journalist Jenaro Villamil described this merged media/government combination as a "reality show" that bore little or no resemblance to the reality that most Mexicans had to deal with in their daily lives.[191] Trying to understand what this reality show represented was like trying to fit the pieces of a mixture of jigsaw puzzles together, none of them complete and with no indications of what the picture should look like.

Although few actually believed in the reality show, it nevertheless cloaked multi-billion peso transfers from one fund to another, government agreements with private investors, entrepreneurs, and drug corporations, greasing the skids for control of business ventures, exchanges of favors for property, high-salaried positions for wives, brothers, children, and falsified environmental and health services reports.

Throughout Mexico, journalists, economists, academicians, and human rights advocates verified what Don Luis expressed: The media dominated national politics (the media defined as the television duopoly of Televisa and TV Aztec, their radio outlets and the major Mexico City dailies). The television giants in particular reflected the policies of Mexico's ultra-conservative Action Party (PAN)

---

189 He asked that his name be withheld "because I can't afford economic repercussions."

190 Retired business owner Luis De La Vega, among others, chided me for this assertion, insisting that the reverse was true: The federal government reflected the views of the television duopoly.

191 Jenero Villamil during the presentation of his book *Si yo fuera president* at the Feria de Libros in Oaxaca, November 2009.

government. Two major issues besetting Mexico—the economy and organized crime—"are like characters out of [the novel] *Pedro Paramo*—ever-present specters, ghosts, oppressive realities that make life difficult, if not impossible," journalist Oscar Rojas told me.

They were oppressive precisely because the government operated *debajo el agua* ("under the water," i.e. clandestinely, underground). On the surface, one perceived only the reality show; the important activity remained hidden from view.

"[For the federal government] the problems always come from outside and debate with the citizenry ends with popularity surveys," Villamil insisted.

3

One of the newly formed PRI's first priorities in the 1940s was to undermine the country's major labor unions, which the Mexican constitution had set up as a counterbalance to the executive and judicial powers. So effective was this infiltration that several unions, notably the Workers and Farmers Revolutionary Confederation (CROC for its initials in Spanish), became unofficial administrators of *debajo del agua* strong arm tactics. They acted as strikebreakers, vote getters, and private security forces for federal and state governments. Like most under-the-water operatives, they were paid in cash, and the payments were disguised in official financial accounts.

Since the few opposition parties that existed before the 1980s had minimal impact on either local or national affairs, the PRI was able to create an alternative government by putting extra-official matters under party control. To many, the PRI and the government were synonymous, but the PRI, as a shadow government, could do many things that PRI government officials couldn't do legally, such as dictate the distribution of government subsidies.

Social programs like providing fertilizer to farmers, milk to children, and rural road construction were channeled by the party to those who voted for the PRI or participated in PRI activities and demonstrations. Groups or localities that failed to conform received nothing. The federal government recorded expenditures distributed to state and local organizations, and they in turn receipted acknowledgements of monies paid out without mention of any groups that had been excluded. Thus everything on paper was *apegado a la ley* ("fixed to the law"), but since the distributions were administered by the party, not the government, those responsible for the expenditures could deny knowledge of any favoritism or private political agreements.

The billions of dollars deposited in Fobaproa (Fondo Bancario de Protección al Ahorro—Bank Fund for the Protection of Savings), which shifted debts owed to Mexico's banks by failed businesses from the private to the public sector in 1994 and re-categorized as the Institute for the Protection of Bank Savings (IPAB) four years later, remained inaccessible in 2007-2009 to jump start the economy and provide employment for thousands of Mexicans driven out of work by the 2007-2008 world economic collapse. According to a retired Mexico City bank investigator that I spoke with, the government transferred nearly US$800 *billion* of taxpayer money to keep the banks solvent.[192]

Many of these bank debts resulted from unsecured loans to phantom corporations that recorded the funds as "salaries and expenses" paid to corporation employees. The corporations promptly disappeared, but bankruptcy laws prevented legal authorities from recovering monies devoted to "employees," even though the employees were the phantom corporations' executives. Since Fobaproa's and IPAB's financial dealings were protected by banking secrecy laws, all transactions occurred *debajo el agua,* as were details of 160 million dollars that the government "purchased" from the banks in 2009 to keep them afloat and the people who they were supposed to be serving in debt.

---

192 The former investigator refused to allow his name to be published.

4

Loyalty has always been more important in Mexican politics than either intelligence or competence. Government positions go to the best *mapaches* (raccoons, as operatives who make sure that candidates win local and state elections). The PRI's 2006 presidential candidate, Roberto Madrazo, rewarded Oaxaca governor Ulisés Ruiz, for what Oaxaca newspaperman Pedro Matias called "his dirty work," by shepherding Ruiz up the governmental ladder, seeing that he became a deputy in the Oaxaca assembly, then a state senator. Ruiz voted the way Madrazo ordered and was unflinchingly loyal to the party. In 2004, he grabbed the gold ring. Oaxaca became his fiefdom to do with as he wished.

Financially, he did extremely well despite the inconvenience of having to deal with the rebellious teachers' union; he had the backing of Mexico's president Calderón. Assassinations, arbitrary arrests, paramilitary "death squadrons," and disdain of human rights organizations not only were accommodated but supported by military intervention while federal authorities assured international wire services and political leaders that unruly mobs had been "contained" and the situation in the state "normalized."

Since legislators cannot be reelected but depend on their political organizations and political bosses for appointments to administrative posts or candidatures for other elective offices, they seldom bite the hand that feeds them. In 2010, when it became obvious to the PRI governor of the state of Puebla, Mario Morín, that an opposition coalition was going to dominate the formerly heavily PRI legislature, he engineered changes to Puebla's state constitution that transferred responsibility for approving expenditures, many of them controversial, during Morín's final year in office. This maneuver cancelled possible efforts by the newly elected legislature to determine the legitimacy of Morín's financial dealings.

It also demonstrated how shrewdly politicians could manipulate laws and procedures to their financial advantage. The no-reelection reform included in Mexico's

135

constitution of 1917 was designed to prevent elected officials from establishing long-term bases for corruption, but in twenty-first-century practice, it encouraged "get-rich-quick" obedience to caciques and governors like Ruiz and Morín. But the 1917 reform did not substantially strengthen the legislative structure; consequently, the latter lacked much of its ability to provide checks and balances against the executive and executive-controlled judiciary. Under both PRI and PAN, non-cooperative legislators were shunted into the background while party loyalists occupied chairmanships and important committee posts.

The influence wielded by *plurinombres*, both in their parties and in the legislature, overrode what post-revolutionary idealists had intended to be a "citizens quorum," which brought farmers, lawyers, business persons, manufacturers, etc., into the lawmaking body. By the 1990s, the competition to be named a *plurinombre* became as intense as the electoral campaigns. The competing parties shuffled those to be rewarded on ladders of preference with both aspirants and the public aware of who was number one, number two, etc.

Thus, governors and other state and party officials whose popularity had ebbed—or who faced possible criminal charges for corruption or mishandling of funds—could continue their political careers without facing voter approbation by becoming an appointed *plurinombre*. The 1917 constitution granted immunity from prosecution to those holding congressional seats, an inducement for the parties to deter investigations for three years (or longer if the person involved achieved another "safe" seat).

During the Fox and Calderón administrations, inspections of safety and labor regulations virtually ceased. Federal authorities overrode reported violations like those that contributed to the Pasta de Conchos disaster in Coahuila and declared the protest and strikes there illegal, thus enabling Grupo México—a major campaign contributor—to resume operations with replacement workers. Similar concessions were made to other major campaign contributors, particularly the television duopoly that was instrumental in defeating liberal candidate López

Obrador's challenge to Calderón in the presidential elections of 2006.

Like the PRI had done in 1988, when supposed computer breakdowns reversed candidate Cuauhtémoc Cárdenas's winning margin over Carlos Salinas de Gortari, Calderón edged past López Obrador after corrections to supposed "computer irregularities" were made. Television newscasters announced Calderón's "victory" before the results had become final (and while López Obrador reportedly held a slim lead over the PAN candidate), announcements later verified by the IFE.

"The same scenario, different names," those of us in Mexico watching the televised reports told each other.

For over half a century, the PRI manipulated election returns, now and then ceding a few benefits to opposition parties from the left and the National Action Party, which was strongly pro-Catholic, on the right. An anti-PRI coalition headed by Cuauhtémoc Cardenas almost toppled the PRI regime in 1988 in an election that Cardenas seemed to have won but that was awarded to the PRI thanks to computer tampering and destroyed ballots. The PAN's candidate, Manuel Clothier, reacted publicly to the results before Cárdenas did. Four days after the election, Clothier called for a national civil disobedience movement that included blocking the international bridges between Mexico and the United States as well as many of the principal highways and boycotting Televisa, the major television outlet, whose very own Jacobo Zabludovsky had broadcast Salinas de Gortari's victory before it became official.

Six days after Clothier called for a national protest, Cárdenas led a Mexico City demonstration. PAN and Cárdenas's National Democratic Front (FND for its initials in Spanish) tried to force a recount, but the Mexican army, apparently under orders from lame duck President Miguel de la Madrid, restricted access to the millions of marked ballots. The PRI-dominated House of Deputies later ordered to have them burned, thus eliminating any chance for future inspection of the disputed results.

Cardenas refused to challenge the House of Deputies' decision, and the newly elected Carlos Salinas de Gortari named several prominent members of PAN to cabinet and administrative posts in exchange for the conservative party's cooperation with his plans to push the North American Free Trade Agreement and other pet projects through Mexico's Congress.

Salinas de Gortari's questionable election wasn't the first in Mexico's post-revolution history. In 1929, outgoing president Plutarco Elías Calles tapped Mexico's ambassador to Brazil, Pascual Ortiz Rubio, as his successor, knowing that he could manipulate Ortiz Rubio and effectively retain control of the country's politics. When popular and charismatic José Vasconcelos, the "Maestro de América" who founded Mexico's public education system, mounted a campaign in opposition and garnered enthusiastic support, Callas called out the army.

Armed soldiers presided over ballot boxes and vote counting and Callas's government declared Ortiz Rubio the winner. On the day of his inauguration, Ortiz Rubio survived an assassination attempt that crippled his left arm. Soldiers and police rounded up twenty-three of Vasconcelos's supporters and executed them near Cuernavaca, Morelos.

The dye had been struck; the one-party "democracy" retained political control for the next seventy years.

When change finally occurred in 2000, it scarcely altered the federal government's overall functions but ruptured the tight vertical system of state and municipal governments that the PRI had developed. Even PAN senator Diodoro Carrasco acknowledged in 2010 that presidents Fox and Calderón failed to "invent new ways of doing things"; consequently, corruption continued unchecked and failed anti-drug corporation policies resulted in the loss of over 50,000 lives during 2000-2010.

5

An incumbent party in Mexico has a great advantage over its opposition, because it can use government employees, including the police, to coax, bribe and strong arm its quest to stay in power. PRI functionaries routinely hustled bags of cement, edibles, and other "inducements" to rural communities to assure that they would vote correctly. Theoretically, such inducements were illegal and sometimes triggered confrontations between the PRI and opposition parties, but all of Mexico's political parties engaged in similar practices, points out Guadalupe Loaeza in *La comedia electoral*. (One of the first things Loaeza was asked as she was putting together her campaign to run for the House of Deputies from the Federal District was "how much can you spend for each vote?")[193]

Although PRI candidates Francisco Labastida in 2000 and Roberto Madrazo in 2006 lost presidential elections to PAN opponents Vicente Fox and Felipe Calderón, PRI governor candidates won elections in the majority of Mexico's thirty-two states and a majority of seats in the national Senate and House of Deputies. The PRI also controlled most state legislatures, enabling it to authorize expenditures for a variety of programs (agriculture, school, highway construction, health services, etc.) that it often failed to fully fund. The money that wasn't spent wound up in *cajas chicas* ("little cash boxes") to be used for keeping party candidates in office.

Even when construction projects were opened to competitive bidding, a governor and/or his public works director could grant the rights to friends or political associates. This one party dominance reduced most state legislatures and the federal Congress to yea-saying compliance. Since the executive controlled the budgetary process, he or she could award no-bid contracts or designate excessive amounts, part of which the supposed recipient never received. Instead, it went into the executive's *caja chica*.

This set up a domino effect where the contractor's accounts would show excessive payments to suppliers and/or subcontractors whose books would show similar overages paid for raw materials, labor, or expenses with each participating business or agency skimming the differences between what the books showed and what actually was paid out.

For a price—often a very high price—a governor could grant land and business concessions, manage a state's

---

193 Guadalupe Loaeza, *La comedia electoral* (2009).

finances without being audited, appoint judges and department heads, and construct a network of acolytes to funnel everything from parking meter collections to drug cartel quotas through his hands. Corruption, whether benevolent or cruel, became the order of the day. Mexican law made no provisions for recall; a governor's access to wealth was virtually unlimited, and the wealth was shared with the political organization that ushered him or her into office.

"It endangers everything," Oaxaca artist and political activist Hugo Tovar shook his head as we conversed on the roof patio of his home in the city of Oaxaca's historical district. "Once accepted, once practiced, it seeps into every crevice. Nothing happens that isn't affected by it."

This "seeping" became very evident in Oaxaca in 2010 when several state educators investigated the actual costs of a huge amount of kitchen equipment that the state Institute of Public Education (IEEPO) had acquired to give as Christmas gifts to persons and entities that had been instrumental in supporting the Institute's education programs. They discovered that the actual cost of the purchases was fourteen *million* Mexican pesos less than IEEPO had recorded. Where did the fourteen million pesos go? Obviously into the pockets of those who had access to the funds and the bookkeeping. That such blatant malfeasance with only minimal cover up could occur demonstrated why politics is a good career, not just for elected officials but bureaucrats as well.

President Calderón gave free reign to the Mexican military to commit abuses in the name of "preserving democracy" while crushing labor movements, restricting journalists, and raising taxes. Similarly, drug corporation *capos* gave free rein to their underlings' hit squads to assassinate competitors and migrants, appropriate agricultural land and suborn politicians and police. To a 2008 survey of what young people in Mexico perceived as their best opportunities to become well off financially, a large percentage of those participating answered "organized politics or organized crime," because both careers promised lots of money and one didn't have to study to achieve them.

Besides that, some added, the *capos* contributed to their communities of origin.[194]

"The poor always are going to be poor and the rich always are going to be rich," a state policeman told a nineteen-year-old after beating him and throwing him into a pickup to be hauled to prison during the November 25, 2006, intervention in the city of Oaxaca. That division between rich and poor has been the guiding principle of Mexico's political system since Spanish *conquistadores* entered the country in the sixteenth century. They allowed the *indigena* communities to govern themselves according to traditional *usos y costumbres*, to weave blankets and grow corn and beans, and to fight with their neighbors but not to share the state's wealth or participate in its financial growth.

Elections in Mexico, like in the United States, cost money—lots of money. By law contributions to Mexican political campaigns from non-governmental sources were strictly limited; the federal government allotted funds to individual political parties for campaign purposes.

Like many well-intentioned laws, this one didn't work in practice the way it was designed to function in theory. Instead of strengthening the electoral process, it stimulated a scramble by half-a-dozen newly formed political organizations to achieve the 2 percent of the popular vote necessary to qualify for federal funding while the major parties—PRI, PAN, and the fragmented remains of the PRD —invested generous federal allotments to propaganda, salaries, and suborning regional caciques. Once their funding was approved, these parties—major and minor— had free reign to spend the money as they chose with minimal restrictions and only rudimentary accounting of expenditures.

"*Un político pobre es un pobre político*" has been a guiding principle in Mexican politics since the 1940s. Officeholders drew exorbitant salaries and benefits in comparison to their counterparts in the United States or Europe. Reelection was prohibited, but running for another office at the end of one's term was not; career politicians

194 Heriberto Ruiz-Ponce, *Noticias, voz e imagen de Oaxaca,* December. 24, 2010.

frequently moved from one elected or appointed position to another, focused on pursuing personal gain rather than serving their constituency.

Although both appointees and regularly elected federal lawmakers showed up now and then in the areas they represented, the majority of them actually lived in the Federal District. In many states, open primary elections were shunted aside and party bosses *"dedazaron"* ("fingered," i.e. named) candidates without input from the constituencies. As a consequence, a candidate needed to ingratiate himself or herself to those making the *dedazos.* Politicians holding elective or appointed offices continued to be *mapaches* for other offices.

In the 1970s, the PRI responded to criticism of its nearly 100 percent control of federal and state legislatures by amending Mexico's constitution to include supplemental delegates and senators in the federal and state congresses based on the percentage of votes that each party received. These *"plurinombres"* were safe seats since those filling them did not have to run for election. This enabled party leaders to reward loyal operatives (often ex-governors, party officials, and relatives of one or the other) by naming them to legislative positions. Virtually all committee heads in both the federal Senate and House of Deputies became appointees, not representatives who were elected by popular vote.

During the 2009 mid-term elections for senators and congressmen, a number of Mexican academics and intellectuals, among them award-winning authors Lorenzo Meyer and Sergio Aguayo-Quezada, advocated the casting of blank or mutilated ballots. They theorized that a million or more of these *"votos nulos"* would force politicians to reassess their political participation and respond more closely to their constituencies. Unfortunately, these academics and intellectuals, like their counterparts in many other countries including the United States, based their theories on ideals and logic, not *mapache* reality.[195]

---

195 *Mapache* (literally "raccoon") was a name given to political operatives who hustled votes for upcoming elections. Those able to bring in winners were often rewarded by being named to high-paying government positions. Some *mapaches,* like Ulisés Ruiz in

The PRI encouraged *voto nulo* balloting in areas that previously had supported opposition parties. The more than a million blank and/or mutilated ballots, which probably would have gone to non-PRI candidates, increased the PRI's winning margins in low participation elections. Party leaders celebrated by pushing increased disbursements to PRI governors through the federal Congress.

After the 2006 national presidential elections, apparently won by the PRD's Andrés Manuel López Obrador but rewarded to PAN's Felipe Calderón, despite assertions of fraud reminiscent of Salinas de Gortari's "victory" in 1988, PRI and PAN operatives convinced a number of PRD leaders to form a dissident movement to diminish López Obrador's popularity.

The federal election board, controlled by PRI and PAN appointees, threw out the results of a tumultuous PRD election marred by multiple irregularities in 2007 and ordered it to establish a second—and more disciplined—process to choose the party president. Dissident Jesús Ortega won, and thousands of PRD stalwarts bolted to other minority parties, shattering liberal opposition to PRI-PAN control of federal policymaking.

Although *voto nulo* voting did not promulgate political reforms or prompt those in power to be more responsive to public sentiment, the million-plus mutilated and blank ballots cast during the 2009 midterm elections (and the high percentage of those eligible to vote who did not) revealed how negatively the voting public regarded the nation's politicians.

"I won't vote for any professional politician," asserted *Proceso* columnist Sabina Berman when she was approached by an election official. "The professional politicians ought to find out that we're not cabbage heads, Teflon skillets, amnesiacs."[196] Berman rejected the frequently cited PRI mantra "shoes are for shoemakers, politics for professionals" by insisting that politics belonged to the people, not to professional politicians.

Oaxaca, rose through successive offices and became governors.
196 Guadalupe Loeaza, *La comedia electoral* (2009).

Like many Mexicans that I talked to, Omar Cosme didn't distinguish among political parties or political programs when he described what "the government" or "the politicians" did or didn't do. An Oaxacan who spent years working in the United States, he regarded government and elected officials in both countries as faceless abstractions, something one had to deal with but couldn't change any more than one could change the weather or the ocean. In a similar vein, in Juan Carlos Rulfo's documentary film *Los que se quedan*, a returned *indocumentado* accused the president of lying 80 percent of the time, then shrugged, "But I don't blame him. That's his job"—as though lying were a preexistent normal state of affairs for elected officials.

Mapache and *karaoke* practices "have converted politics into a bad reality show and threaten to transform elections into a badly produced performance by telegenic figureheads."[197] The end justified the means even though, in the words of former PAN congressman Jesús González-Schmal, "on the way, principles, independence, dignity, and the nation itself are scattered to the four winds."

6

Scattered to the four winds with them were support of the arts and of education. To the privatization-committed *panistas*, "culture" was an exploitable enterprise whose worth was defined by how much revenue it brought in. Year after year they trimmed government funding to arts projects, theater, the movie industry, and liberal arts education, but funded multi-billion dollar spectaculars like the one on September 15, 2010, commemorating the bicentennial of the Mexican revolution.[198] Under *panista*,

---

197 Jenaro Villamil, "Los políticos karoake," *Noticias, Voz e Imagen de Oaxaca,* September 9, 2009. Villamil used the term "karaoke politics" to describe officeholders and appointees who sang the *"canto de jefe"* ("chief's song").

198 In keeping with Calderón's elitist philosophy, access to Mexico City's Zócalo where the celebration was held was restricted to invitees—predominately government and business figures. Calderón on national television urged the rest of the population

Presidents Fox and Calderón's archeological and historical sites (including Teotihuacan and the Basilica of the Virgin of Guadalupe) incorporated five-star hotels, shopping malls, spectacular light shows and pyrotechnic displays, golf courses, and guided tours that altered history to conform to business interests and conservative philosophy.[199]

As detailed in Section III, many of those in power regarded literature and art as suspect because both had incubated liberal theories. The murals of Siquieros, Orozco, and Rivera depicted revolutionary themes, as did the writings of Carlos Montemayor, Julio Scherer-García, José Joaquín Blanco, and others. Mexican theater productions and films aroused similar suspicions, both because of their political themes and what conservative Catholic leaders considered "immoral" presentations of human relations, particularly nudity and sex.

"It would appear that there's a [federal government] initiative to eliminate theater and convert it into a specter or mere memory," concluded *Proceso* columnist Estela Leñero-Franco after seeing Calderón's proposed 2011 budget, which further reduced federal support of the arts.[200]

Theater in Mexico was becoming an "elitist" camaraderie of a few government-supported grant recipients, she insisted, much like the arts had been under the dictatorship of Porfirio Díaz in the nineteenth century. "Culture" in officialese indicated adherence to traditional values (often mythologized to ludicrous proportions) and

---

"to view the celebration on television." And despite the fact that it was a national holiday celebrating the independence of Mexico from foreign control, the contract for presenting the spectacular was given to an Australian entrepreneur.

199 "The government assaults our traditions. It grossly and insultingly commercializes our culture and openly intervenes in communities that do not bend beneath its demands. It violates the *indigena* communities that according to their traditions seek forms of coexistence and self-determination. The government refuses to recognize the will of the people and fractures community life by imposing its authoritarian practices." *Declaration of the Peoples of Oaxaca,* August 2006.

200 Estela Leñero-Franco, "Teatro," *Proceso,* October 10, 2010.

not to innovative programs that developed citizen participation.

Curtailing the arts, particularly theater and cinema, increased a dependence on imported products, technicians, and artists. The major movie theater chains distributed U.S.-made films and rejected Mexican-made movies, even those that won awards at international festivals.[201] Mexico reverted to being a supplier of talent and locales for foreign-made films; many of its major directors, photographers, and actors migrated to the United States (another example of outsourcing, according to Toby Miller of the University of California in Riverside).[202]

Because the "culture" defined by contemporary art, street theater, political stencils, community radio, documentary films, and small-press poetry editions perverted establishment propaganda and went against the prevailing philosophy of worth defined monetarily, the government's enhancing of Mexico's archeological wonders (like enhancing its primeval beaches, selvas and lagoons) with five-star hotels, golf courses, multi-dimensional light shows, and super highways became "cultural," while reading Nobel Prize poets, attending controversial theater exposes, or watching a sunset illuminate life-teeming mangrove expanses was "counterproductive" and did not serve the goals of the establishment.

Different = bad; conformity = good. All that one needed to know, one could absorb from television, a disgruntled magazine editor described governmental attitudes towards creativity.

7

So embedded in the political system had corruption become that persons like Carlos Beas in Oaxaca who took stands against it faced prosecution. Beas and "a small

---

201 Cinépolis, Grupo México (Cinemax and MM Cinemas) and Cinemark owned nearly 87 percent of the theaters and registered nearly 94 percent of the cinema income in 2009. The three major chains operated in conjunction with U.S. distributors.

202 Vértiz de la Fuente, Columba, "¡Ya basta!" *Proceso,* August 15, 2010.

group of teachers, indigenous peoples, community leaders, and professionals" published an underground newspaper in which they denounced the abuses of the government and rich landowners whose *pistoleros* had assassinated a number of local leaders who had opposed the takeovers of *indigena* lands.[203]

The group's efforts generated enough of a following that local strongmen, apparently with the blessings and support of the *priista* state government, jailed, killed, or forced community organizers to flee their villages, much as state police and paramilitaries retaliated against the Oaxacan popular movement in 2006 when activists confronted armed military and militarized police with slingshots and marbles. An Oaxacan alternative media journalist told me the following in 2008:

> He [Governor Ulisés Ruiz] has the police and the guns and the arrest warrants and the money. We can march and shout and curse, but it doesn't do any good except maybe to make us feel a little bit better. Some, I know, have talked about assassination as the only way. Armed revolution. But we don't have arms. It would be shooting marbles out of slingshots at Robocops armed with R-15s. And nobody but us cares. Nobody in the rest of Mexico cares. Nobody anywhere else in the world.

Beas fled Mexico twice to avoid being imprisoned, and numerous participants in the newly formed Union of the Communities of the Northern Zone of the Isthmus (UCIZONI) were jailed or assassinated. Nevertheless, UCIZONI's opposition to the expropriation of *indigena* lands forced the government to abandon plans to construct a highway from the Isthmus of Tehuantepec to the newly developed tourist mecca in the Bay of Huatulco, but "in other places the resistance of the pueblo was isolated, therefore quickly defeated."[204] Much of the self-sustaining

---

203 Carlos Beas, *Teaching Rebellion*, ed. Diana Denham (2008).
204 Ibid. Mexican law theoretically granted *indigena* communities the right to confirm or negate development of the land they occupied, but particularly in southern states of the republic, government officials and entrepreneurs routinely bribed local caciques to

farming in southern Mexico gave way to plantations of eucalyptus for pulpwood and African palms for palm oil; denuded hardwood, oak and pine forests became grazing land for herds of beef cattle as the markets for coffee and oranges diminished and Mexico began importing "terrible quality cheap yellow corn."[205]

Continuing resistance to mega-projects devised by foreign interests that were pushing millions of dollars into Mexico also derailed the "Plan Puebla-Panama," an ambitious NAFTA-linked scheme encompassing highway construction, land development, and free trade agreements that would have tightened U.S. economic control over southern Mexico and Central America. Community activists, primarily *indigena,* and the Zapatistas in Chiapas, physically and through legal challenges blocked land takeovers for highway construction and the controversial venture withered. It was reintroduced on a smaller scale as the "Mesoamerica Project" in 2008.

The US$950 million that the United States intended to pump into the Mesoamerica Project theoretically would have boosted the local economy—if it didn't disappear into the pockets of those responsible for purchases and construction. *"Sin obras no hay sobras,"* ("Without construction projects, there aren't overages"), another of PRI mover-and-shaker Carlos Hank-González's quotable slogans,[206] was a guiding principle throughout Mexico, from the ill-fated super library commissioned by President Fox, to state and municipal road and housing construction.[207] Legislators and governors campaigned on

obtain rights to construct engineering and hydroelectric projects or, through federally ordered expropriation, to back up acquisitions with military force. Although Mexico had environmental protection laws and regulations for insuring that they were obeyed, those responsible for approving the environmental feasibility of projects belonged to the same power coteries as those financing and benefiting from them.

205 Ibid.

206 www.gurupolitico.com/.../el-pez-por-su-boca-muere-las-150-frases

207 Jenero Villamil, "Despilfarro," *Proceso,* March 18, 2007. The Biblioteca de México José Vasconcelos, an expenditure of 2 trillion 300 million pesos, became a white elephant the day it

the merits of past and future highways, bridges, agriculture, and potable water, the federal government included financing in its budget projections, the money was appropriated, but all too often the projects never were implemented because of incomplete *tramites* (required procedures), costly studies that may or may not have taken place, or the funds were diverted for election purposes or other uses.

President Fox's much ballyhooed cement floors for rural homes project was marred by reports that contractors colluded with government inspectors to dilute the cement-sand ratio when installing the floors. They then sold the unused cement powder for additional profit. The floors soon began to break apart, crumble under the weight of furniture or footsteps, and lose their texture, leaving sandy residue. Acapulco artist Esther Vázquez copied a federal audit report that revealed that in the state of Guerrero, local officials and local contractors embezzled nearly Mex$150 million from the cement floors project.[208]

Other scams perpetrated by government-allied private contractors included highway projects that failed to comply with guidelines for roadbed construction or used inferior and less costly materials than authorized. Others diverted diesel, vehicles, and manpower to other uses. Roads that should have lasted for ten or twenty years crumbled from lack of maintenance and shoddy construction. Citizen protests usually evoked more promises than results, although, occasionally a government agency filed charges against an alcalde or municipal president for graft or misappropriation of funds; however, prosecution, if it occurred at all, typically wound up strangled by legal challenges or bureaucratic procedures and few convictions occurred.[209]

---

was inaugurated in 2007 and immediately had to be closed for renovations and repairs.

208 Phone conversation with Esther Vázquez in December 2009.

209 Frequently citizens and citizen groups and those charged with official audits recognized corruption by governing officials but lacked documentary proof. A case in point: In 2008, Oaxaca state auditors investigated a municipal president for embezzling funds but were unable to establish how he had accomplished it since no paperwork—receipts, contracts, etc.—existed. The

That politicians controlled the government rather than the government controlling politicians made objections to such things as construction bids illusory. It also created and/or supported a power structure that made it indispensable that the party in power retain its political dominance or face audits and/or criminal charges for misuse of funds, failures in the justice system, and other irregularities.[210] Even when changes occurred, they usually involved a re-accommodation of those in the ruling elite, not a visible change of policy or politics.

An exception was Cuauhtémoc Cárdenas's election to become the mayor of the Federal District in 1998 and the subsequent election of Andrés Manuel López Obrador as his successor in 2002. That the latter sought to identify himself with the citizenry rather than the ruling elite promulgated charges that he was "a danger to Mexico" when he ran against Vicente Fox in the presidential election of 2006, "Mexico," in their definition, being the political establishment.

8

As described in the previous section, organizing unified opposition to governmental/entrepreneurial takeovers was sporadic and seldom permanent. Governors, federal officials, and drug corporation *capos* always seemed to have enough money to achieve land acquisitions, elections, drug exportations, patents and other extralegal acquisitions.

Since the Spanish Conquest began in the sixteenth century, foreign powers, first from Europe then from the United States, played major roles in maintaining a flow of raw materials out of Mexico and suborning the country's leadership to "Westernized" local control in the hands of wealthy entrepreneurs and business leaders. In 1925,

---

official went on to become director of a state civil protection agency.

210 Rafael Barajas, "El Fisgon," pointed out during his Oaxaca appearance that corruption by governors or presidents typically remained hidden until an opposition party gained control and conducted audits and criminal investigations.

Robert Lansing, U.S. secretary of state under President Calvin Coolidge, declared that Mexico was an easy country to dominate, because its political power was concentrated in the hands of one individual: the president. Consequently, the United States should open the doors of its universities to young Mexicans who could work their way into influential political positions and eventually assume the country's presidency.[211] Mexico's presidents from 1982-2000—de la Madrid, Salinas de Gortari and Zedillo held Mexican-funded doctorates from U.S. universities.

After World War II ended, Mexico wavered between developing fledgling industries and agriculture that had begun to prosper during the war years or responding to U.S. pressure to export the bulk of its raw materials, particularly oil but also cotton, copper, and other products. Economists Daniel Cosio-Villegas, Frank Tannenbaum, and Emilio Uranga advocated government involvement with local small producers and farmers to form auto-sufficient "mini-economies" and farming cooperatives that would provide employment and stem the rural-to-urban flow that was congesting Mexico's cities and impoverishing already strapped outlying areas.[212]

But fascinated by and envious of U.S. prosperity, the country's leaders focused on imitation and television- and movie-propagated, post-war lifestyles. Money from the United States brought results more quickly than money generated by renovating outmoded industrial and agricultural equipment and systems of operation. Although most Mexicans continued to assert their belief in traditional Mexican values, especially those that involved local customs and Church celebrations, they did so wearing Western clothes, watching television, and getting divorced.

Long before the "invasion" of transnational firms like Walmart, McDonalds, and Home Depot, supermarkets,

---

211 The almost monarchial authority vested in the president (and in governors) also fostered corruption since the executive didn't have to respond to legislative, judicial, or popular criticism.

212 www.estudioshistoricos.inah.gob.mx/.../historias_29_121-130.pdf.

department stores, and shopping centers were becoming commonplace in Mexican cities. With the massive migration of workers to the United States, rural as well as urban residents learned to consider electric mixers, women's jeans, chainsaws, and hamburgers as necessities for everyday life.[213]

Governmental campaigns against corruption have occupied headlines for the past eighty years. So has U.S. condemnation of this same corruption. But throughout this period, those condemning and campaigning have been entwined in the intricate web they purportedly have been trying to break. The United States has strongly supported Mexico's patriarchal system of government for economic reasons, backing executive control of policymaking, particularly oil exports and arming the federal military to combat drug exports. Simultaneously, the U.S. government has refused to legislate arms sales or deal forcefully with the internal market for cocaine, marijuana, smack, and designer drugs.

The U.S. State Department's assessments of human rights violations have had more to do with political alignments than with actual events; they annually list countries with left-leaning governments as the principal violators and sugarcoat the apprehensions, assassinations, and impoverishment of dictatorships and pseudo-democracies like Mexico and Colombia. Numerous sources have indicated that the United States financially supported Felipe Calderón's presidential campaign against López Obrador in 2006. Although hard data about purported support is lacking, U.S. campaign experts participated on Calderón's behalf, and the United States promptly recognized Calderón's controversial victory over the "leftist" PRD aspirant.

More damaging to Mexico's poverty-wracked millions has been profit taking by the U.S. and multi-national firms that assumed control of Mexico's banks, agriculture, and industry after the passage of NAFTA. Foreign-owned banks in Mexico registered greater profits for their stockholders than those stockholders realized in their countries of

---

213 Robert Joe Stout, "*A Dónde* Mexico?" *America,* February 22, 2010.

origin, largely because the foreign firms enticed those responsible for Mexico's banking regulations—specifically the executive and legislative branches—to grant enormous concessions and minimize restrictions. Bogus loans of millions of pesos, phantom corporations and financial institutions, and here-today, gone-tomorrow investment firms, both Mexican and foreign, profited as the country's financial system crashed in the 1990s, taking with it hundreds of thousands of individuals and small industries and businesses.

The green light given by NAFTA to U.S.-backed mega-corporations and agribusiness to "Walmartize" huge swaths of what formerly had been successful (or at least functional) small agriculture and industry, thrust millions into poverty, increasing the outflow of currency that no longer would be available for local investment and reducing labor to a non-unionized temporary (and poorly paid) workforce. In the process (with the cooperation of local caciques and politicos) the NAFTA-backed entrepreneurs polluted wasterways and transformed formerly productive land into flood plains and grazing land.

Their actions—and attitudes—were not that much different from U.S. G.I.s and college students who crossed the border to get drunk, buy drugs, and/or go to whorehouses: "Who gives a damn about the people—or the country—as long as we get what we want?" The doors for corruption were open and foreign investors, principally U.S., Canadian, and Spanish, became major practitioners. Like their Mexican counterparts, they kept most of their dealings *debajo del agua* while presenting surface morality. The business practices and financial dealings that many foreign investors and entrepreneurs adopted would have netted prison terms if the perpetrators had attempted them in their home countries.

As Ugo Codevilla, Federico Campbell, Miguel Ángel Granados-Chapa, and many others have pointed out, when a country's business, social, and political leaders visibly engage in corrupt practices, the majority of the citizenry, accepting that such practices are sanctioned, also become corrupt, and no amount of patriotic bluster—either from Mexico City or Washington, D.C.—changes that dynamic.

SECTION V - ECOLOGY

1

During the second half of the nineteenth century, Mexico "enjoyed" what President (Dictator) Porfirio Díaz boasted was productive economic and social advancement. Foreign investment brought the construction of railways and established profitable mining, manufacturing, and agricultural exportation. This investment did not, however, abolish or diminish racial and social segregation. Only ten percent of the population of sixteen million could read and write; ninety-five percent of the wealth was in the hands of the ruling aristocracy.

The revolution (actually revolutions) of 1910-1926 decimated the economy and reduced the country's population by more than 10 percent. Although the country established a "revolutionary democracy" influenced by both the U.S. system of government and that of the newly formed socialist government of Russia, the country's ruling elite continued to maintain dominant economic control. Nevertheless, they responded to twentieth century demands for better trained, literate workers and administrators by establishing public education, which hadn't existed during the *"Porfirato"* of the preceding century. They also placed limits on the Church's political power and on foreign participation in the economy.

The nationalization of Mexico's petroleum industry in 1938 temporarily deflated exports to the United States, but after the United States entered World War II, it turned to Mexico and Latin America for oil, minerals, cotton, livestock, coffee, sugar, and other products no longer available from Europe and Asia. European intellectuals, scientists, educators, and engineers sought refuge in Mexico and established businesses, industries, and schools. The rural-to-urban flow increased, creating demands for services and housing—demands that were met in improvised and uncoordinated fashion as squatter settlements multiplied and mass acreage crops replaced individually owned small farms.

Throughout this time of expansion, U.S. interests and ideology were at work. The Rockefeller Foundation-funded "Green Revolution" promoted agricultural advancement but encouraged private investment in the north over self-sufficient agriculture in fertile southern states (Oaxaca, Chiapas, Tabasco) where abundant summer rainfall and ecological conditions that eliminated the need for chemical fertilizers enabled farmers to harvest three corn crops a year. This productivity vanished with the appropriation of farmlands for cattle grazing more suited to northern Mexico. Legislation promulgated by large landowners eliminated acreage restrictions on land devoted to livestock enabling regional caciques, members of the "noble elite," and moneyed investors to transform huge acreages of fecund agricultural land to raising livestock for export.

The *cardenismo* of the post-revolutionary years centralized the majority of productive activities; as a consequence, those in the federal bureaucracy making major decisions concerning agriculture frequently lacked the knowledge and experience of local farmers and farm administrators. That many federal secretaries of agriculture had more political than agricultural experience (and belonged to the political and moneyed elite) contributed to decisions overly influenced by investment possibilities and individual career advancement.[214]

The imposition of U.S. values—wheat over corn, huge acreages instead of small home-owned farms—"failed to compensate for the amounts of money invested," insisted Gustavo Esteva.[215] The Green Revolution's attempts to

---

214 Anecdotal but apparently true, a federal agriculture sub-secretary, after examining aerial photos of Sinaloa rice fields, urgently telegraphed state officials demanding they report the damage caused by the "destructive flooding" he'd just viewed. (Conversation with Demetrio Antonio of Mazatlán, Sinaloa.)

215 Gustavo Esteva, Beatriz Canabal, and Fernando Rello, "Formas y relaciones agrícolas" in Josè Gutiérrez-Vivo, coordinator, *El mexicano y su siglo* (1999).

induce an inappropriate system of agriculture impoverished more people than it fed, although a handful of modern *hacenderos* profited enormously and assumed political and economic control of the northern states of Chihuahua and Sonora.

2

With the enactment of the NAFTA free trade agreement with the United States and Canada, Mexico's federal government accelerated the privatization of former public functions, including the use of ground water and aquifers. Overexploitation for industry and uncontrolled urban growth "has gravely stressed" the nation's water resources, Octavio Rosas-Lando told *La Jornada* during a reunion of the National Assembly of Those Affected by the Environment (ANAA). He insisted that governmental actions violated the country's environmental, water conservation, and property ownership laws, and announced that the ANAA had registered a formal demand against the Mexican government with the Latin American Water Tribunal.[216]

ANAA recognized what many governmental supporters of free trade agreements seemed to ignore: the agreements increased commerce (and profits), but simultaneously drove a wedge between haves and have-nots in both the exporter and importer countries. They also tacitly encouraged collateral movements that included worker migration and export-import of non-legal goods like cocaine, heroin, and sophisticated weaponry. Those on the free trade bandwagon prospered, but in their wake left hundreds of thousands (if not millions) of un- and underemployed, a degraded environment, and diminished natural resources.

Like many offshoots of accelerated growth, proliferation of solid and chemical waste increased exponentially with the implementation of NAFTA. Rivers and estuaries became contagious currents of contamination as oil drilling

---

216 Octavio Vèlez Ascencio, "El gobierno mexicano destruyó el sistema hídrico, afirma la ANAA," *La Jornada*, September 12, 2010.

destroyed wildlife, and sewage ruptures in overstressed urban areas deposited chemical, fecal matter, and industrial waste in the diminished water flow. Millions of plastic water and soft drink bottles, whose production had been encouraged by the federal government but for which no recycling programs existed, clogged sewers and drains and provided breeding pools for hordes of mosquitoes, including those carrying the deadly dengue virus.[217]

Although individual communities fought to preserve self-sustaining and ecologically renewing modes of living, Mexico's federal government gave only token acknowledgement to protection of the environment. Mexico's three U.S.-educated, neoliberal presidents stressed the development of the Bolsa de Valores and guaranteeing high profits for Mexican-affiliated transnational businesses. The North American Free Trade Alliance opened Mexican markets for U.S. exports by eliminating tariffs and guaranteeing favorable conditions for investors. Mexico became even more a U.S. subsidiary shoving cheap raw materials northward and importing foodstuffs and manufactured items.

Laura Carlson of the Americas Policy Program of the Center for International Policy affirmed in 2007 that the NAFTA trade agreement crippled agriculture in Mexico, citing Oaxaca's Mixteca region as an example:

> After centuries of misuse, the land suffered from one of the worst erosion rates in the world and chemical farming had depleted the soil. Then, lower yields were combined with the impact of increased imports under NAFTA that drove the domestic price of corn down 59

---

217 In the late 1980s, I witnessed a scene not untypical of the way that governmental authorities dealt with congestion and what they termed "environmental contamination." During a stopover in Iguala, Guerrero, my stroll along an unpaved road was interrupted by a flotilla of motorcycles and convoy of old trucks filled with uniformed state police. From the top of a slope, I saw the police fan out among a squatter village of several hundred ramshackle dwellings, most of which seem to be constructed of corrugated metal, car parts, cardboard, and thatch. With clubs, hatchets and machetes, the police tore the dwellings apart and hurled butane stoves, beds, tables, chairs, and wash tubs—and a little girl's tricycle—into the trucks and hauled them away.

percent between 1991 and 2006 ... today the Mixteca region of Oaxaca has one of the country's highest rates of out-migration ... In Nochixtlan a farmers' organization has built trenches to stop erosion, started a reforestation program that has planted three million native variety trees to date, and instituted sustainable farming techniques ... But they need help, U.S. trade policy sent these communities into deep crises.[218]

In 2010, Mexican farm organizations insisted that given needed governmental support—loans, storage, irrigation, and security against organized crime—Mexican growers could produce enough corn to feed 200 million people. But the federal government, committed to economic policies that courted foreign investment, focused on raw material exportation and increasing importation of agricultural products, joining other former agricultural product exporting countries as importers of food and grain.[219]

Aware that geographically and environmentally Mexico couldn't equal the mass acreage grain production of the United States, groups of *campesinos* and rural townspeople organized small cooperative production facilities and credit unions to re-form depleted communities by incorporating former government functions into their *usos y costumbres* social systems. Many of these *campesinos*—probably a majority—had worked in the United States and brought modern agricultural concepts with them when they returned to Mexico.

However, they couldn't totally emerge from the past through modernization. The Spanish conquerors had governed through a thoroughly organized system of satrapies, empowering local caciques with economic and political control. These caciques—*ladinos, mestizos, indigenas*—became little kings with the power to distribute

---

218 Laura Carlson, www.americaspolicy.org, text based on a Congressional briefing on NAFTA presented December 6, 2007.

219 By 2010, less than a dozen transnational corporations controlled over 50 percent of the world's food supply as the bulk of agricultural exports shifted from the southern hemisphere to the northern hemisphere.

wealth and resources however they chose as long as they paid the required tribute (goods, labor, soldiers) to the crown.

The Spanish administrators did not consider agricultural production particularly important. Spain was producing a sufficient quantity of food to feed its inhabitants and didn't need to import from a continent thousands of miles away; the *conquistadores* wanted gold, silver, lumber. But as a minority submitting a huge land area and hundreds of thousands of residents to its control, many of whom spoke languages different from one another and who had been webbed in internecine hostilities for centuries, the Spanish felt it necessary to impose a political structure modeled after those in vogue in Europe.

As more Europeans pushed into Mexico, they established Spanish-type towns with wall-to-wall structures facing narrow streets leading to a governmental square and central marketplace. They did not recognize communal property, but instead gave individual titles of ownership to land that had previously been communal dwelling areas. Many *indigena* communities were forced to relocate to the fringes of the new population centers or establish home sites in outlying areas. The European overlords, accustomed to beef and mutton as mainstays of their diet and horses as their primary means of transportation, appropriated vast acreages for grazing, taking possession of communal land that they considered to be un-owned, hence unoccupied.

Conflicts between the Europeans and the native populations erupted throughout the three centuries that followed the conquest. Most of them involved land use and governing authority over the areas in which the *indigenas* lived.

These European systems of ownership and government remained virtually unchanged after Mexico gained its independence from Spain. The elite that assumed political control exploited natural resources, transforming self-supporting, agriculturally-dependent residents into wage-paid—and often abused—laborers. Mexico became—as it is today—an exporter of raw materials and a consumer of imported food and manufactured goods.

Although individual priests and missionaries treated the *indigenas* as "brothers," the Church hierarchy merged with the landholding aristocracy. The wealth it manifested in the construction of Medieval-style cathedrals in the major metropolises of Mexico to "inspire" the native popular to believe in their God contributed to the separation of the ruling class from the *indigena* and *mestizo* population. Missionaries accompanied the *conquistadores* and encouraged the native population to accept and convert to the European religion whose customs and practices they seldom understood. "Converting" meant more than merely accepting a new religion, it meant subjugation to foreign authority, religious, political, and economic. It meant a loss of dignity, of a way of life.

"You—not you of course, personally, but those from your culture who advocate the marvels of this 'super chief' have created what you define as the 'Indian problem,'" a Tojolabal *indigena* named Aurelio Rodríguez told me in Chiapas. He goes on to say,

What you don't understand is that we are not a 'problem.' We have a problem: you. You and your super chief god are the problem. Your insistence that there is something wrong with the way the Tojolabales have lived since long before your people knew about guns or engines or airplanes.

Our struggle is not for conquest. We do not need to rusticate you. We do not care if you and your people worship your 'super chief,' even though we see that it only makes you angry, only makes you want more of what you already have too much of—oil, gold, coffee beans. It is to have back a way of life that is rich with contentment that we struggle.[220]

3

Throughout the revolutions and counter-revolutions that began in 1910, the *revolucionarios*, particularly those led by Emiliano Zapata and Pancho Villa, demanded the

---

220 Robert Joe Stout, *The Blood of the Serpent: Mexican Lives* (2003).

breakup of huge plantations and haciendas and restoring the land to *campesinos.*[221] Unfortunately, the latter failed to achieve the independence they'd envisioned after the establishment of a new government based on the constitution of 1917. Bare subsistence living typified rural life as urban centers grew and industrial infrastructure and exportable agriculture dominated the country's leaders' political programs. María Dolores Paris-Pombo defined the situation in post-Revolution Chiapas:

> The expansion of the exportation of prime materials was a secure investment for a few families when coffee, cacao, sugar and hardwoods began to offer very attractive prices in European markets. In Chiapas a few palatial centers constituted a tiny imitation of European life with imported art, clothing and all the luxuries of elite provincial life.[222]

The pioneer spirit of "intrepid adventurers taming the wild" who pushed into the forests and jungles, created plantations, probed the Earth for oil deposits, blasted right of ways for roads and railroads persisted throughout the last half of the nineteenth and first years of the twentieth century. Part-time university professor Jesús Richter described his German forbears in conversations I had with him in San Cristóbal de las Casas, Chiapas, as the following:

> For the Germans, I'm convinced, Mexico represented the dark side of the id with all of its energy and flamboyance and sensuality. One only has to read Freud to learn how repressed they were, how little they indulged their dreams. They were obsessed with order—so obsessed they didn't have any *duende* in their lives. By cutting the jungles, driving out the primitive forces, they were harnessing the id. I think a lot of these Conradian characters didn't make it—harnessing the id. I think a lot of them lost themselves in it. They got

---

221 Villa's forces often fought only during the winter and returned to their farms to plant and harvest, forcing Villa to reconstitute his army every year.

222 María Dolores París-Pombo, *Oligarquía, tradición y ruptura en el centro de Chiapas* (2001).

eaten by the dragons that came out of the jungles—or out of themselves, I don't know which.[223]

Most major emigrations from Europe to the New World, Africa, and the Near East to Europe, the Boers to South Africa, Hispanic America to the United States, were triggered by necessity, not romanticism or choice. Immigrants filled vacancies that existed—in farm labor, construction, manufacturing, and technology; they did not necessarily resume the roles they'd vacated in their places of origin. Colonial Mexico, established by adventurers— *conquistadores*—entrepreneurs, royalty—lacked the industrial revolution middle class prevalent in Western Europe. Famine in Ireland, political turmoil in Germany, debtors' prisons in England, wars, revolutions, droughts, religious persecutions—plus armies of occupation— brought thousands of tradesmen, laborers, educators, speculators and farmers to Mexico in the late eighteenth and nineteenth centuries. They followed where opportunity led them—to farm, manufacture, construct, teach, sell, or steal. Another descendant of German immigrants to Chiapas told me that

Coffee beans aren't perishable like pineapples, like mangoes or bananas or pears. The market was there. We didn't invent it. When we came into the industry, there was a demand for coffee. It's not possible to grow coffee in the United States. It's not possible to grow coffee in Europe. We gave the world something it wanted. It was our work, our identity, our … it was *us!*"[224]

Like so many things in business, in manufacturing, in farming or education—or for that matter in government— the identity created by fulfilling a need was swept away by changed circumstances, just as the lives of the *indigena* farmers was permanently altered by the political conquest of the land with which they identified.

---

223 Robert Joe Stout, *The Blood of the Serpent* (2003).
224 Ibid.

4

For years the environment as defined by forests, waterways, and wildlife seemed to resist—if not overwhelm —the intrusions being made by explorers and entrepreneurs. Environmental rules and regulations were slight, and even where defined, were disregarded.

More sources of lumber existed than could be harvested, the *selvas* seemed endless, the mineral deposits unlimited. Except in northern desert areas, water was pure and plentiful. The challenge was to tame, change, exploit, create a "Nueva España" modeled after life in France and Spain, a Nueva España defined along racial grounds. The *criollos—blancos*—along with a smattering of *mestizos* composed a ruling elite that controlled government, the economy, and religion. They resisted any possibility of merging into *indigena* Mexico or adopting any *indigena* customs or beliefs.

This modeling surged dramatically after Porfirio Díaz assumed the presidency in the latter half of the nineteenth century. Díaz and the "*cientificos*" of the entrepreneurial-governmental coterie pushed industrialization and the establishment of infrastructure for commercialization and transportation, particularly railroads that connected all of the outlying regions with Mexico City. French, English, Scandinavian, and U.S. immigrants established workshops and bakeries, polo and cricket associations, Parisian and Italian clothing outlets, hospitals, private schools, and universities.

Society became increasingly Creole—light-skinned, with the creation of a three-tiered caste system in which the elite controlled manufacturing, government, and the economy, *mestizos* provided the bulk of the labor and the *indigenas* were relegated to serf-like servitude. All values except European values were considered "inferior"; the political challenge was to Europeanize the *indios* since their ignorant and "savage" or superstitious ways negatively affected Mexico's growth into a modern (i.e. European-style) nation.

The denuding of the Selva Lacandona in Chiapas took thousands of *indigena* lives as lumber barons enslaved native workers to cut and export hardwood. Newly constructed railroad lines split communal lands and forced indigenous inhabitants to migrate to the less productive sierras. *Mestizo* and European newcomers established a monetary system that triggered inflation.

Similar to what was happening in the United States, a newly forming middle-class gradually pushed its way between the autocratic overlords and the *peones,* although it developed slowly and did not spread to rural areas. This newly forming middle-class, though participants in the "taming of the wild," was not per se rapacious. Many "mini-*hacenderos"* acquired small sections of land and planted orchards, raised vegetables more typical of European than Mexican diets, and started small businesses that hadn't existed previously. They built roads, installed small-scale irrigation projects, and established dairies, tanneries, brick making, and various professional services. Although they evinced similar prejudices towards the native population as the U.S. middle-class did towards Native Americans, much of what they did was ecologically sound.

The revolutionary turmoil of 1910-1926 turned everything topsy-turvy. The European middle-class orchardists and shop owners had little reason to join the revolution, nor did they have any reason to defend the *porfiristas.* When things finally calmed down, the new government had almost nothing—political power, yes, but not typewriters nor milling wheels nor canneries nor clocks. The agrarian reform and the nationalization of the oil industry provided openings for mechanics and merchants and schoolteachers and people who could make bread and shoes and plows and cement. In fact, it created the very thing that Marxist revolutions supposedly deplored: a conservative petite bourgeoisie.

Between 1910 and 2010 Mexico's population expanded from approximately sixteen million to nearly 110 million. In 1910, over 80 percent of the population lived in rural areas; in 2010 over 80 percent were urban dwellers without the potential to produce their own food. Great expanses of formerly productive growing areas had been desolated by drought and erosion. Landowners and entrepreneurs in many areas shifted to raising livestock or replacing food-producing land with export crops: coffee, cotton, sorghum, and other types of livestock feed, eucalyptus for pulpwood, and African palm for palm oil.

By the year 2000, the country needed to produce eight times more food than it had a century earlier, but its ability to do so lessened with each passing year. Imports increased and with it the economic and political power of what Confederación Obrera Revolucionaria director Angel Oliva-Solís termed the *"burguesía de invernadero"* ("greenhouse middle-class"), an urban elite motivated by financial gain at the expense of self-sustaining agriculture.[225] Small landowners and *campesinos,* unable to modernize as U.S. farmers had done, remained mired in the past without the financial resources to rent or purchase modern planting, irrigation, and harvesting equipment and unable to obtain credit or loans.

> If we import more food than ever before it's because the government is dedicated to having it that way: that we dedicate ourselves to buying food from the exterior, that our function in the world scheme of things is to be purchasers of food, not producers.[226]

Statistics presented by the Universidad Autónoma de Nuevo León during a 2009 conference on nutrition in Chile defined over twenty million Mexican residents (nearly 20 percent of the population) lacking access to adequate food. Areas with the highest percentages of extreme hunger spread across southern Mexico—Guerrero, Chiapas, Oaxaca, and the highlands of Pueblo, Jalisco, and Durango —but also included the barrios and *colonias populares* of most major cities.[227]

By 1994, the federal government had withdrawn subsidies on fertilizer, diesel, and other necessities, eliminated the Conusupo markets that had offered low cost

---

225 Arturo Romo-Gutiérrez, *Última frontera* (2003).
226 Gustavo Esteva, Gutiérrez-Vivó coordinator, *El Mexicano y su siglo* (1999).
227 Bulletin issued by the Asociación Mexicana de Bancos de Alimentos dated October 2009.

goods to rural residents, Agrosemex that had provided seed, and Banrural that had issued government guaranteed loans repayable after harvest.[228] Although the country continued to be the world's fourth largest grain producer, it was forced to import five to six million tons of corn annually. In *La economía política del maíz en México*, Francisco Lelo de Larrea insisted that not only did Mexico lack advanced agricultural technology and infrastructure and little access to financing, but the aid that the government was providing was misdirected.

Instead of targeting increased production, which he termed positive, this aid was being used negatively through anti-poverty programs that provided temporary relief but perpetuated the inability of *campesinos* to modernize.[229] Modernization, he insisted, would include growing corn for ethanol production since the demand for ethanol grains was driving the prices paid for corn higher; with increased profits, farmers could expand both their incomes and production and reassume integral roles in the country's economic and social well-being.

Inflation triggered by increased privatizations and bureaucratic decisions involving importation and speculation drove the prices of basic commodities out of the reach of individual small farmers who received less each year for what they produced.[230] By 2007, the country was importing US$1.5 million worth of agricultural and food products *every hour!*[231] The United States Department of Agriculture predicted in 2010 that Mexico's dependence on U.S. and Canadian imported corn (40 percent in 2010)

---

228 However, the U.S. government continued to subsidize corn production, which enabled farmers to produce crops for less than their Mexican counterparts, consequently making corn imported from the United States cheaper than that grown locally.

229 Francisco Lelo de Larrea, *La economía política del maíz en México*, 2007. In contrast with experts not affiliated with private sector production Lelo de Larrea advocated the use of *"semillas mejoradas"* (i.e. genetically modified seeds).

230 Arturo Romo-Gutièrrez, *Ùltima frontera* (2003). According to Romo-Gutiérrez, in 1990 Mexican agriculture provided 86 percent of the nation's food; in 2000, only 68 percent. That percentage diminished to between 25 and 35 percent in 2010.

231 Laura Carlson, "Drug War Doublespeak," 2009.

would double by 2030 if the country didn't redirect its agricultural policies. These policies, based primarily on political considerations not on research and investigation, failed to confront how increasingly vulnerable Mexican agriculture had become.

By 2010, changing climatic conditions had diminished rainfall, reducing gross agricultural production by 10-15 percent, UNAM's Victor Magaña-Rueda reported.[232] UNAM's director of the Program for Climate Investigation, Carlos Gay-García, complained that the country lacked accurate information about how vulnerable Mexico had become to climatic changes, prompting *El Universal* to pose the question: "If we don't know how vulnerable we are how, is it possible to develop policies of adaption to contingencies of the climate?"[233]

Forested land became desert in various parts of Mexico, stimulating emigration and relegating vast expanses of arable land to cattle grazing and desiccation. (And in some areas marijuana and opium poppy cultivation.) Nevertheless, Mexico's federal government did not alter its 1980's determination to de-emphasize auto-sufficient agriculture.

Mexico's presidents in the late twentieth century determined to reduce the rural *campesino* population from thirty million (nearly one-third of the nation's inhabitants) to a mere five million. Carlos Salinas de Gortari (1988-1994) pushed a constitutional change through the federal legislature removing the restriction on selling *ejido* land before Mexico and the United States confirmed the North American Free Trade Agreement in 1993. (The *ejidos*, created during the administration of President Lázaro Cardenas in the 1930s, were properties deeded "in perpetuity" to landless rural residents.)

When reporters asked one of Salinas's secretaries of agriculture, Carlos Hank-González, what was going to happen to the millions of struggling but self-sufficient farmers being forced off their *ejidos*, Hank-González shrugged and replied amiably, "I don't know. That's not my department." (How much Hank actually knew about rural

---

232 *El Universal,* October 5, 2010.
233 Ibid.

agriculture is questionable. Mexican cabinet posts traditionally were awarded to party faithful whether or not the persons appointed had any knowledge about or expertise in the field they'd been named to direct.)

5

Uncontrolled urban growth during the last quarter of the twentieth century surged across the country, a tsunami that devastated everything in its path, including regulations concerning land use, drainage, sewage, and construction. Colonial cities became industrial slums, law enforcement no longer could control increasing criminality, and emigration became a way of life for millions of Mexicans. Hundreds of thousands of square kilometers of arable lands dried into unproductive dust bowls or sparsely inhabited cattle and sheep ranches.

The vast majority of former *ejidarios* migrating to urban centers scrambled for whatever work they could find to support themselves and their families. Separated from communal roots where roles were clearly defined and where the entire community adhered to the same norms, these newly arrived urban residents had to adjust to purchasing rather than producing their own food, clothing, and household items.

By the late 1990s, rural-to-urban migration had slowed but hadn't abated. Mexico City's phenomenal growth was duplicated by population explosions in formerly provincial cities like Hermosillo, Chihuahua, and Monterrey in northern Mexico. None were prepared or able to offer adequate services, especially to poor workers and their families, many of whom lacked primary school educations and technical skills.

Illegal and dangerous electrical and gas connections proliferated, drainage clogged (where it existed) and *aguas negras* (water contaminated by unprocessed sewage) overflowed through streets and into the subsoil. "All of the country glows with the absence of collection and secure treatment of solid waste from the cities, commerce, and industry," complained environmentalist Iván Restrepo.[234]

6

As Mexico's population grew during the colonial and post-colonial periods, forested lower slopes gave way to agriculture, particularly in areas near the seacoasts. Nevertheless, early twentieth century paintings and photographs show most Mexican cities surrounded by green expanses. But distinctions between legal and illegal blurred as timber, mining, hydroelectric power, and land takeovers affected individual communities and entrepreneurs.

By the late twentieth century, modern logging equipment enabled well-financed impresarios to register enormous profits in many parts of the Sierra Madres where lumbering had been previously difficult. Although Mexico's National Commission for the Use and Understanding of the Biodiversity (Conabio) reported that Mexico had lost 30 percent of its forests and *selvas* (tropical forests) during the last half century, lumber proponents insisted that the country boasted one of the hemisphere's largest reserves of unharvested timber.

Investigators probing the devastating floods that inundated nearly a third of the southeastern state of Tabasco in 2007 determined that hurricanes and tropical storms had been part of the state's climate for thousands of years, but heavy growth in the higher elevations had deterred excessive flooding. As grazing land and urban development replaced wooded areas, rainwater poured into the Río Grijalva and other waterways and swept through towns and cities on its way to the Gulf of Mexico.

Mudslides wiped out entire villages in Chiapas and *colonias populares* in Mexico City and Monterrey, the result of unchecked growth that had denuded forest-covered hillsides. Over one million hectares of forest disappeared every year.

---

234 Ivan Restrepo, "Nuevo Leon," *La Jornada,* August 9, 2010.

National Air and Space Administration (NASA) photos taken for the Monarch Butterfly Sanctuary Foundation in eastern Michoacán and the western part of the Estado de Mexico showed clear cut patches appearing throughout areas that contained extensive butterfly colonies. NASA geographer Daniel Slayback told the *New York Times*, "There are a number of sawmills in the area that are busy eating away the forest ..." Neither complaints from within Mexico or from outside induced governmental action. The monarch butterfly population diminished accordingly.

The Monarch Reserve was one of nine areas that Mexico's federal government defined as "ungovernable regions" in which illegal logging was taking place. Mario González-Espinosa of El Colegio de la Frontera Sur in Chiapas described heavily armed groups that raided community and *ejido* forests at night and illegally extracted timber without the consent of owners who avoided confronting them or bringing them before the authorities.[235] (During the past three decades, only Brazil recorded a higher rate of deforestation than Mexico.) Although a large percentage of the logging in Mexico was legal, a gray area existed where inspection and local granting of permits remained unaudited.

Often those hauling the lumber to sawmills had timber cutting permits but not in the areas in which they'd been logging. Other, smaller operators harvested timber in beetle-infested areas after previously damaging a few trees by severing roots and pouring weed killer on them. (The beetles attacked the damaged trees; according to federal guidelines, all trees within the surrounding radius could then be cut.) Federal regulations dictated replanting, but those who cut illicitly did not try to replace the trees they felled. Not infrequently, sawmill owners simply pocketed a

---

235 Elio Enriquez, "Alerta experto sobre acelerado deterioro ambiental en Chiapas," *La Jornada,* July 16, 2007. Also See Neptali Ramìrez-Marcial, Angèlica Camacho-Cruz and Mario Gonzàlez-Espinosa, Guìa por la propagaciòn especies leñosas de las altas y montañas del Norte de Chiapas, undated, for the problems and challenges involved in reforestation projects in Chiapas.

"fee" (i.e. bribe) from the logging companies and processed lumber brought to them without asking questions.

Efforts to thwart unregulated timber cutting foundered until the federal government elevated protection of the environment to federal cabinet status. Even so, the country still "lacks a clear and logical vision of developing the countryside," insisted Fernando Rello of Mexico's National Autonomous University.[236]

"The animals eat more than twenty million *campesinos* put together and have destroyed a fifth of our forests in order to feed them!" Gustavo Esteva expostulated during a roundtable discussion in Mexico City.[237] Nearly 7,000 of Mexico's estimated 22,000 individual plant species have commercial or domestic value and many risked extinction, because their native habitat was being destroyed or they were being harvested without consideration for renewed growth.

Although Mexico's federal and state governments were modeled after U.S. and European systems with executive, judicial, and legislative branches, the majority of the power remained with the executive. Governors ran their states as personal fiefdoms. Despite environmental protection, law enforcement was weak, and individual governors could crack down on illegal logging, overlook or encourage it, or grant concessions to local caciques and have environmental activists arrested or even assassinated. Rural residents of Guerrero's eastern mountains told me that not only the state police but detachments from the Mexican army helped timber takers by harassing and arresting those who objected to clear cutting.

When Mixe residents of the state of Guerrero's high Sierras tried to block roads in the early 1990s to prevent illegal foresters from hauling the lumber they had cut, state police "swept in and beat up people and threw them in jail," a Mixe told me. "Every time we point out something illegal that the lumber cutters are, doing the police arrest somebody." Usually the charges are for assault or

---

236 Fernando Rello in José Gutiérrez-Vivó, coordinador, *El Mexicano y su siglo* (1999).
237 Gustavo Esteva in José Gutiérrez-Vivó, coordinador, *El Mexicano y su siglo* (1999).

destruction of private property, he explained, but sometimes for attempted murder or rape "anything so they can send us to jail."

In February 2010, armed militaries opened fire on men and women working near the community of La Morena, Guerrero, killing one, wounding others, and arresting two community members that they accused of "health crimes," charges usually levied against those in possession of drugs for sale.[238]

In a 2001 report on the country's natural resources, *Proceso* correspondents Raúl Monge and Silvia Ortiz accused the federal government's commission to regulate clear cutting of promoting "nothing short of ecocide."[239] They quoted Environmental Protection Agency head José Ignacio Campillo-García:

> We found incongruities, such as a reduction in the number of forest rangers from 3,000 to 300 and the allocation of more budget money to reforestation programs than to inspection and surveillance programs. All of this makes me think that in former administrations there was a lack of interest and even a deliberate intention to do away with natural resources.

In 2008, nearly 75 percent of Mexico's forest land was communally owned.[240] Many land and ownership disputes that went back centuries remained unresolved and led to violent confrontations, especially when lumbering occurred in areas where more than one community or communal group claimed ownership. The federal government preferred to establish measures that over-regulated forest activities instead of investigating and trying to settle these conflicts. The new regulations impeded local use of forest products, which were environmentally sound, and

238 Internet bulletin sent out by the National Association of Democratic Lawyers (ANAD). ANAD insisted the charges were "fabricated by the soldiers."

239 Raùl Monge and Silvia Ortiz, "Ecocidio," *Proceso,* July 8, 2001.

240 The Mexican Civic Council for Sustainable Forestry listed 60 and 80 percent under community control. Estimates varied because of conflicting claims of land ownership and ephemeral demarcations between communal, government, and privately owned property.

penalized those who had made the best attempts toward preservation and management of forest resources.

Nevertheless, throughout southern Mexico individual communities or communal groups instituted restoration projects. Residents in Ixtlán de Juárez not only replaced forested areas with seedling pines but slowly established local furniture manufacture from native woods. Unfortunately, despite praise and encouragement from international agencies like the Rainforest Project and Forest Stewardship Council, their land management and reforestation project preserved only a tiny islet (approximately 50,000 acres) in a sea of wildcat logging and urban devastation.

7

The federal government's belief that it could enrich the country by fulfilling part of the world demand for oil transformed life in the formerly idyllic states of Tabasco and Campeche. Oil filled lagoons and saturated farmlands and waterways drove thousands of residents into *colonias populares* on the fringes of the cities.[241]

Oil spills not only fouled waterways bordering the Gulf of Mexico, but pipeline breakages and leaks in the interior contaminated streams and destroyed farmland. Diesel filtering into the Río Tula in Hidalgo killed thousands of food and sport fish and the ducks and herons that ate the carcasses.[242] Oil-coated seafowl cluttered the stained inlets around Atasta and other communities bordering the huge Laguna de Terminos in Campeche and Laguna Catemaco in Veracruz.

Nevertheless, drilling continued. New cities like Benito Juárez and Ciudad Pemex surged into being, and established cities like Villahermosa, Minatitlán, and Coatzacoalcos lost their idyllic colonialism and became industrial centers with all the attendant problems of

241 A former Isla del Carmen accountant told me, "There was so much oil in the water that you could lubricate a truck with what you could squeeze out of a *huachinango* (red snapper).

242 Carlos Camacho, "Mortandad de peces en Tula por presunta fuga de diesel," *La Jornada,* February 17, 2007.

contamination, traffic, and crime. Landowners along the thousand-mile stretch of hillsides bordering the gulf expanded their holdings to hike production of fruit, vegetables, grains, and coffee. Smaller farmers and orchardists pushed higher into the hills, uprooting *indigena* communities. Even those who warned that the oil wouldn't last forever admitted that life—and the environment—never again could be the same.

8

Frequently, I heard business executives (and the politicians they supported) proclaim, "Mexico needs oil, minerals, timber, or there's no progress!" Even those among them who confirmed "there are disadvantages" insisted on "a balance" between "scenically primordial *naturaleza*" and the needs of industry and commerce. While boasting that Mexico was "multi-cultured," they tacitly (and sometimes openly) encouraged environmental depredations on *indigena* lands leading to conflicts with lumbering, mining, cattle grazing, and the petroleum industry.

Although the land reforms and creation of *ejidos* in the 1930s theoretically diminished the holdings of property barons and *latifundistas,* the latter circumvented the new laws by establishing separate *ejidos* for various members of their extended families—sons, daughters, brothers, cousins, *prestanombres* ("loaned names," i.e. persons affiliated with the *latifundista*).[243] Conflicts over titles took years—often decades—to resolve.

The Cardenas partitioning of land conformed to the feudal philosophy of authoritarian control. The head of the government, the father-figure, the uncrowned king, passed out all dividends. In the 1930s, the dividends passed out by the father-figure were family ownership *in perpetuity* of a piece of land on which to live and, ostensibly, farm,

---

243 José Antonio Cruz, *Absalón Castellanos y los terratenientes, 1982.* For example, in Chiapas, forty-four families owned over a million hectares of farm and grazing land, an average of 23,000 hectares per family while 0.8 percent of productive land was owned by 40.7 percent of the *campesinos.*

although in a majority of cases it was land that had been barren for decades and/or was located in isolated and inhospitable regions.

Ownership didn't materially affect the status quo. *Ejido* dwellers who'd been living in poverty continued to live in poverty. Rural communities, both *indigena* and *mestizo*, lacked the resources that the wealthy and newly forming middle-class enjoyed—potable water, drainage, roads, education, electricity. As had been the system since colonial times—and in some areas pre-colonial under the Mayas and Toltecs—the few benefits received came from above: the governor, president, viceroy, cacique. *Ejidarios* and *campesinos* became even more dependent upon the state and the governing political party. Even those who could produce more than they could use had only government-subsidized consortiums to whom to sell, usually at well below market prices (and often below the cost of production).

The withdrawal of supports by the father-figure, in this case the federal government, lacerated the *ejido* system and the concept of auto-sufficient faming that accompanied it. More and more frequently, individuals and individual communities took environmental matters in their own hands, halting environmentally damaging construction and devastation by blocking highways, mine entrances, taking over administrative centers, etc. ("I'm astonished that there hasn't been more sabotage," Veracruzano Federico Cruz confided to me. "It goes to show how basically decent the people are, and what *pendejos* are those in government.")

9

Mexico's once flourishing fishing industry also demonstrated over-dependence on the father-figure. Many who formerly garnered a livelihood from the sea accused the government of betraying them by withdrawing subsidies and loans while allowing foreign fish factories to deplete the fecund waters of the Sea of Cortez, southern Mexico's Pacific coast and the Gulf of Mexico. By the year 2000, the Pacific fishing fleet consisted of vessels that resembled "rusting equivalents of Model A Fords kept together with axle grease and soldering rods," a Baja California Sur fisherman told me.

In contrast with the glistening computer-driven facilities of the foreign fleet, local fishermen unloaded their catches into troughs of open-to-the-weather gutting and filleting work stations on shore as they'd done for generations. Refrigerated vans, panel trucks, and pickups hauled the catches to markets throughout the country. (Trucks lacking refrigeration loaded the filleted fish in tubs or barrels of ice.) Refrigeration (or icing), transportation, and merchandising ate up most of the profits; the fishermen themselves made next to nothing and government-supported entrepreneurs imported huge quantities of domestically-farmed salmon from Chile and African food fish from European and U.S. importer-exporters.

The disappearance of protective coral reefs—natural barriers against storm-driven floods and land loss as well as an extensive close-to-shore habitat for fish, shellfish, and vegetation—accelerated during the last decades of the twentieth century. Scientists belonging to the International Coral Reef Initiative attributed much reef damage to "natural causes": climate change and temperature modifications that provoked over-acidification of ocean water but also from the expansion of seaports, tourist facilities, water contamination, over-fishing, and the destruction of mangroves lining bays and coastal waters.

Increased water temperature caused the algae on which coral fed to die, with the result that the reefs calcified and also died, leaving only fragile remains easily broken apart by storms. In some areas, like Cozumel off the coast of Quintana Roo, implementation of artificial reefs reinforced existent reefs and kept them alive, but in other areas calcification and mangrove removal to accommodate tourist facilities greatly endangered coastlines, harbors, and ports.

"If we destroy them (coral reefs and mangroves) it wouldn't surprise me that Cancún could disappear" as the sand washed away and rising sea levels covered the popular resort, insisted UNAM's Roberto Iglesias.[244]

10

Throughout Mexico, environmental impact reports glossed over possible infractions and approved mining, construction and lumbering projects that clearly—visibly—damaged the environment. Nevertheless, both the government and transnational corporations boasted about supporting the environment and pointed to regulations and policies that they'd promoted or endorsed without referring to statistics that showed more mining concessions being granted, more reefs and archeological sites being deformed, and more forests being denuded. To top it off, drug corporations added lumber production as one of their sources of income in order to make former forest land available for marijuana and *adormidera* cultivation.

Both the federal government and entrepreneurial class found it practical to bypass or ignore environmental restrictions rather than openly oppose them. Mexican authorities signed international environmental accords but did not defend federally designated "Ecological Conservation Zones" against encroachments.

Officials from Semarnat, the federal agency responsible for environmental protection, applauded Jalisco governor Emilio González-Márquez's public announcement that the state had acquired thirty-six kilometers of coastline that included portions of a federally protected sea tortoise sanctuary. Members of the University of Guadalajara's Sea Turtle Conservation Program denounced the acquisition as illegal and demanded that 1986 accords establishing the

244 Angèlica Enciso L., "Destruido en 29 años" *La Jornada,* April 14, 2009. Iglesias linked deforestation with reef destruction, explaining that erosion pouring into the estuaries strongly affected the composition of sea water and caused the reefs to asphyxiate.

sanctuary be obeyed. But anticipated profits from the proposed mega-development took precedent over environmental protection measures.[245]

When I asked a veteran correspondent from a Mexico City daily why these encroachments were allowed to happen, he hooked his forefinger close to his thumb in the Mexican gesture for *lana*—money. Those running the government (i.e. entrepreneurs who opened doors to wealth for politicians who contributed to increases in entrepreneurial power, control, and financial gain) extolled hydroelectric projects that increased energy production but drove domestic prices for services higher, promoted genetically modified corn that purportedly increased per-acreage production but forced small growers to conform or lose their land and the destruction of shrimp and food fish estuaries, coves, and coastline to install tourist facilities that profited investors more than shrimping or fishing could.

Massive publicity campaigns accompanied the approval and inauguration of mega-projects in which the government was involved. Governors, senators, cabinet members, even the presidents of the republic, lauded accomplishments and benefits on prime time television. Commentators and news broadcasters described entire communities that rose in protest as "dissident minorities" or "gangster-led violators" and tagged protest leaders with criminal pasts without mentioning that their "criminality" involved participation in anti-government demonstrations.

---

245 This abrogation of environmental laws reminded me of northern California loggers who demanded "since when is a goddamned redwood more important than a human being?" during a 1980s interview. Mexican and foreign developers expressed similar sentiments in arrogating environmental regulations for private purposes. Profepa inspectors in Quintana Roo in 2001 reported illegal occupation of beachfronts along the state's 538 miles of coastline by Mexicans and foreigners who'd established restaurants, services, and residences. That same year, Profepa reported that not a single investor bothered to request authorization from federal authorities to build on or occupy beach areas in Nayarit. As happened with the sea turtle sanctuary in Jalisco, vows to crack down on abuses slid by the wayside as profit took precedence over protection.

Not everyone in government—or every governmental entity—benefitted from these mega-developments. Municipal authorities in the Baja California port of Ensenada closed the transnational corporation Sempra Energy's liquid natural gas facility for violating environmental regulations that included discharging contaminated waste into the Bay of Ensenada and for violating regulations that required local approval for the construction of docks and 160,000 cubic meter storage tanks. Sempra officials and Baja California politicians who'd facilitated the company's operations vehemently denounced the bursting of this bubble, which Ensenada officials insisted was designed to deliver coastlines, waterways, territory, natural resources, and financial gains to Mexican functionaries and foreign entrepreneurs behind the back of the citizenry.[246]

Rather than attempt to eradicate the contamination of the Río Santiago in Guadalajara, Jalisco's metropolitan area, federal and state authorities authorized a three-billion five hundred thousand peso expenditure to divert waters reeking with industrial waste for commercial and industrial use by constructing the Arcediano dam. Nine years and Mex$700 million later, the government of Jalisco cancelled the project because the river, one of the most polluted in the country, had become even more contaminated and because geological conditions in the Barranca de Huentitán increased construction costs to nearly five times the original appropriation.[247] Undaunted, state authorities thrust weight behind another hydroelectric project, "El Purgatorio," which would

246 Jaime Martínez-Veloz, "Sempra Energy y la carabina de Ambrosio," *La Jornada*, March 11, 2011.
247 Both the contamination and the geological fault were well-known and well-advertised in 2002 when the project was designed and approved. At least one state engineering official who questioned the viability of the Arcediano project was dismissed from his position. Citizens displaced by the project finally achieved a demand for revision. As a result, the state environmental management department determined after investigation that the original evaluation was inadequate and lacked official written approval by the federal government.

inundate the town of Tamacapulín and the surrounding area.[248]

Those in power frequently responded to criticisms and revelations about past and potential ecological damage by counterattacking environmental regulations and those who tried to enforce them ("the best defense is a good offense"). Or they called for "negotiations" and promised studies and evaluations by experts that often took months or years to complete.

Typical of such evasions occurred in Hidalgo in 2009 when Governor Ángel Osorio-Chong solicited expert opinions and promised thorough investigations and negotiations after residents of Zimapám blockaded the depositing of toxic materials in a 135-hectare rented landfill in 2009. The contaminating operations continued while investigations were being made and proposals were being discussed, modified and further studies and investigations undertaken. Osorio-Chong's government lauded its dedication to the nation's ecology, but the contamination continued.[249]

A 2009 tuberculosis epidemic in Chiapas spread despite the state's efforts to counter it, because turgid bureaucratic regulations and the appropriation of health funds for other purposes gutted their efforts. Despite the catastrophe, the government of Chiapas continued to boast about its appropriations for ecological causes without detailing actual expenditures (a subterfuge practiced by politicians throughout the world, including those in the United States).

Throughout Mexico, collusion between entrepreneurs and public officials sabotaged protests against mining ventures, tourist mega-developments and hydroelectric projects. As occurred to those actively objecting illegal lumber taking in Guerrero and the Estado de Mexico, arrests and assassinations subverted protests against the Canadian mining firm Blackfire in Chiapas, the huge

---

248 Miguel Concha-Malo, "Asignaturas pendientes," *La Jornada,* December 26, 2009.

249 Carlos Camacho, "Impiden vecinos ingreso de explosivos con aparente destino al basurero de Zimapàn," *La Jornada,* April 14, 2009.

Pichachos dam project in Sinaloa, and the El Zapotillo dam in Jalisco.

Replacing whistleblowers and/or non-compliant engineers or other experts paved the way for private investors to inaugurate or continue construction detrimental to the environment (also a tactic not exclusive to Mexico). Even when appeals courts ruled in favor of protesters who'd been arrested and were serving prison sentences, so much time had elapsed during the appeals process that the projects had been totally or substantially completed by the time the verdicts were registered. Individual government authorities diverting complaints about violations or ecological damage by denying responsibility for a particular activity thrust clarification onto the judicial system with similar results.

The presence of drug organizations in project areas, electoral campaign waffling to keep from antagonizing either pros or cons among the voting public, and the inability of federal, state, or local budgets to contribute prescribed support further complicated ecological determinations. Even governmental approval of environmental restrictions didn't assure compliance; comprehensive studies often outlasted the governmental terms of those initially involved in their formulation.

The failure to care for natural resources, especially forests and farmlands, was closely tied to urbanization and migration. Extensive lumbering denuded areas surrounding cities in the country's interior; rural residents abandoning (or driven off) self-sufficient, small farms accelerated erosion, and their move to urban areas overwhelmed sanitation facilities, contaminated water, and provided cheap labor for ecologically unsound industry.

The purported War on Drugs and linked security issues sapped the federal treasury, causing the government to diminish funding to the support and administration of clean industry, potable water, drainage, and reforestation. Corruption—not just governmental but corporate bribes, tax evasion, and suborning local officials—subverted environmental laws and regulations.

Crushing protest movements as "criminal" perpetuated this corruption, as did uninvestigated assaults and assassinations. The U.S. government advocated "green zones" and ecotourism in Mexico but simultaneously promulgated toxic waste disposal sites and increased importation of petroleum, just as they financed and trained the Mexican military while supporting—and sometimes originating—shipments of automatic weapons to the drug corporations.

"In politics," a professor of mine told me years ago, "there are no good guys or bad guys. Just practical, possible, and convenient." And there are no isolated political issues. They are intricately interconnected. Tap one strand of the spider's web, and the entire structure vibrates.

After the record rainfall that hurricane Alex hurled against northeastern Mexico in 2010, government authorities in Nuevo Leon estimated that the reconstruction of dwellings, schools, and governmental buildings, roadways, and communications systems would cost an estimated 17.5 billion pesos (approximately $1.2 billion U.S. dollars). But the state government signed an accord with Femsa, one of the nation's largest construction conglomerates, to build a new football stadium on parkland in Monterrey, the capital of Nuevo León. Not only did construction require extensive changes to traffic patterns, it destroyed the ecological buffer that the park provided against further flooding and industrial contamination.[250]

"Who needs a roof over one's head if one has a football stadium?" an unemployed Monterrey office worker asked me after describing the state governor's pronouncements about how magnificently the stadium would benefit Nuevo Leon's citizenry.

Both Monterrey and the city of Oaxaca were devastated in 2010 by flood waters surging through what had been described as "dry rivers" from which water for irrigation and industrial uses had been diverted. Storm-swollen mountain streams and gullies poured into river beds clogged with debris and garbage that blocked the waters passage, creating flows that ripped across densely inhabited lowlands. Cutbacks in funding for basic services,

---

250 Ivan Restrepo, "Nuevo León," *La Jornada,* August 9, 2010.

often blamed on "the economy" but frequently caused by deviation of funds to retain power and win political elections, urban expansion that replaced green areas, parks and clear-cut forest lands with asphalt and concrete, and the lack of enforcement of established environmental norms transformed streams, barrancas, and farm and orchard lands into "*basureros* [garbage dumps] that swelter with vermin, toxic poisons and fecal waste," a frustrated Oaxaca legal administrator told me.

11

During our conversations in Chiapas, Jesús Richter confided, "I am afraid that eventually Mexico will become two countries. One will be like the United States with McDonalds's burgers and computer screens and Santa Claus, and the other will be a huge human garbage dump where all the *indigenas* and the refugees and the displaced and poor people will live."

A venerable *curandero*, also from Chiapas, lifted a crooked finger when I repeated what Richter had told me and gestured towards construction that had begun on an ambitious new tourist complex encroaching on the excavated temple at Palenque, the marvelous highlands capital of the Mayas in Chiapas that had been abandoned and had disappeared beneath tangled growth long before the *conquistadores* arrived in the New World. Slight of build but clear-eyed, with wrinkles around his mouth that seemed constantly on the verge of a malicious grin, he peered past the earthmovers and I-beams, cement mixers and power generators towards lush growth on the hills behind the ruins. The wind had diminished to a mere whisper, and the rainy mist clinging to the hills sparkled goldenly in mid-morning sunshine.

"To build the next 'Palace of the Gods,'" he told me in his quiet lisp. "And when the gods abandon them all this will disappear. As it did before it will disappear again."

Seeing the oil spills, the denuded hillsides, the ravaged cities of northern Mexico and the abandoned towns and villages in the south, the steel girders and slag piles of rock and sand bleaching in the sun as the country slid into overwhelming debt, social violence and division of resources between the rich and the poor that exceeded all previous dimensions was enough to make one believe that the gods had already abandoned this nation of 110 million people.

The jungle was taking over again.

CONCLUSION

1

If the landmines are there, why hasn't one exploded before this?

Despite the two countries contrasts and differences, an uneasy adhesion existed between the two. Politically, Mexico's current and past administrations maintained stability and power with the backing of the U.S. government—and billions of dollars that accompanied that backing. The United States was Mexico's primary market for oil exports, agricultural, and manufactured products, and U.S. firms not only exported automobiles, computers, and movies but, thanks to NAFTA, established manufacturing plants, service businesses, and retail outlets within Mexico itself.

By 2010, 12 percent of Mexico's active workforce lived in and labored in the United States; before the economic fallout of 2008, they contributed almost as much as oil exports to Mexico's economy through remittances to their communities of origin. That families—and communities—accepted being divided between two countries and two cultures created cultural bonds that were not visible to lawmakers responsible for immigration decisions. Mexican-born citizens in the United States maintained many traditions and values of their homeland while simultaneously adopting new ones. Through the constant interchange of persons and material goods, those in Mexico absorbed U.S. ways of doing things.

In much the same manner, Mexico's governing elite absorbed U.S. ways of doing things while ostensibly maintaining national integrity. As previously noted, three consecutive Mexican presidents held PhDs in economics from Ivy League universities. They and the political party to which they belonged, the PRI, endorsed free market theories being pushed by the United States and by countries of Western Europe. They lowered protective barriers after the North American Free Trade Agreement took effect in 1994.

They did not, however, go whole hog. "Free enterprise" and "free trade" as values were limited to a narrow economic sphere. Throughout the 1990s and the first decade of the twenty-first century, the United States became increasingly protectionist in areas of broader economic activity: commerce in narcotics and migration spurred by economic needs. Politicians on both sides of the border redefined these latter two economic concerns as separate—essentially non-economic—issues. That enabled them to deal politically and legalistically with them as "criminal," i.e. outside or in violation of free enterprise/free market activity.

Rationally they are not. Morality issues aside, commerce in narcotics follows free market principles: profitably providing a desired product to those who want it. By the same token, undocumented immigration provides a desired product—labor—to those who want it. Spending billions of dollars on protectionist issues while simultaneously denouncing protectionism is self-defeating —hitching horses to opposite ends of a wagon.

The billions spent during the War on Drugs did not materially alter the demand for that product in the United States, nor have the billions spent on battling undocumented immigration demonstrably affected motives for migrating. While those billions were being spent, hundreds of thousands—if not millions—of people in each country tumbled into unemployment, poverty, and debt. The cost of protectionism has been high, and its failures have resulted in tens of thousands of deaths, wanton corruption, and ever increasing personal and public insecurity. Moral issues are woven into economic issues. Separating them may make for simplified legislation, but it does not alter the dynamic.

2

In *Dying To Live*, Joseph Nevins uses the term "MexUSA" to describe communities whose residents are separated by distance but not by identity. The bonds uniting them are as strong, if not stronger, than those that unite the political or commercial entities of the two countries. They also function as an emotional buffer. The same Mexican citizens who abhor U.S. policies, particularly concerning immigration and the War on Drugs, speak positively—even affectionately—about Americans and life in the United States.

Mexican citizens wear the same clothes, buy the same things, voice many of the same opinions, even root for the same athletic teams as their U.S. counterparts. Contentment with "the old ways" eroded as Mexicans developed norms and expectancies that hadn't existed before. Simultaneously the U.S. government (and many U.S. state and local governments) adopted strong anti-immigrant stances but continued to make it possible for agricultural, construction, manufacturing, and service firms to employ seven million undocumented Mexican workers (as well as four-to-five million from other countries).

Immigration seemed not to have figured in the master plan for control of the northern Hemisphere, viewed by the World War II Roosevelt administration as essential for U.S. national security. Making the Gulf of Mexico and the Caribbean an "American Mediterranean" necessitated reducing all the countries bordering the sea—Mexico, Central America, Columbia, Venezuela, and the islands of the Caribbean—to dependency on U.S. policy. The NAFTA and ASPAN (Alliance for Security and Prosperity of North America) treaties, resisted only by Venezuela and Cuba, tightened military and economic control while isolating immigration, the War on Drugs and environmental concerns as separate issues. These issues have become landmines that have threatened to shatter the effectiveness of the master plan.

Creating this American Mediterranean necessitated the cooperation—official or *debajo del agua*—of the nations involved. However, those wielding political power deemed it prudent not to disclose details of the plan to the cooperating countries but gave them nominal liberty to pursue their own interests as long as these interests did not disrupt or threaten the plan's long-term success.[251]

Military interventions kept the Central American countries from sliding away from this domination, but control of Mexico primarily was exercised economically: loans, grants, private and government investment in manufacturing, and natural resources. Mexico prospered but fell heavily in debt to both the United States and to international lending institutions. The debts assured Uncle Sam and the neoliberal financial institutions of continued political dominance.

Circumventing laws and regulations while protesting compliance to them benefitted both private enterprise and the suborned governments; enforcement was directed towards symptoms not the cause of the problems. Many private enterprise manipulations in Mexico were veiled by secrecy laws; many others were condoned or swept under the table by compliant officials who prospered personally from disregarding or falsifying financial and environmental regulations.

Simultaneously, U.S. law enforcement systematically increased clampdowns on undocumented immigration rather than on those hiring them; the War on Drugs physically attacked drug corporations rather than focusing on financial manipulations that lined the pockets of entrepreneurs and government officials as well as corporation *capos*. Laws and regulations became tools of those responsible for administering them, not for providing security for the citizenry or the environment in which it lived.

Maintaining this double standard of surface propriety and *debajo el agua* maneuvering necessitated curtailing or derailing public investigations and protests. Mexico completed the privatization of its banking system, begun under Carlos Salinas de Gortari in the 1990s, by transferring multi-billion dollar bank debts to a government fund, the interest on which had to be paid out

---

251 Nicholas J. Spykman, *America's Strategy in World Policy* (1942).

of taxpayer dollars. All investigations of fraudulent investments were cancelled, and the fund was protected from public audit. The banks, the majority now foreign-owned, took advantage of Mexico's less restrictive banking laws to levy fees and charge for transactions that far exceeding what their home countries legally permitted.

The War on Drugs, intentionally or not, provided the U.S. further means to exert control. Military armaments, helicopters, hi-tech surveillance and detection systems, trainers and DEA agents filtered into Mexico. Mexico's president, Felipe Calderón, pushed increasingly restrictive laws through Congress and the House of Deputies while granting impunity to the armed forces that had replaced civilian authorities combating the so-called cartels. The United States, meanwhile, only superficially acknowledged the popularity of drugs among its populace and made only token attempts to limit arms manufacture and export.

Seldom discussed in either Mexico or the United States were the economic benefits garnered by the transportation and sale of cocaine, marijuana, and designer drugs. Luxury item purchases, condominium sales, tourist resorts, airlines, auto and airplane sales and sports franchises absorbed billions of dollars flowing into the marketplace. Phantom financial and investment groups whisked money through offshore banking systems. Stock markets prospered. Over 70 percent of the money in circulation in Mexico originated with or involved the commerce in drugs, according to most estimates.

Estimates varied, but most attributed over 70 percent of the money in circulation in Mexico in 2010 derived from commerce in narcotics.

Debajo de agua both governments were aware that ending the drug trade would end prosperity for hundreds of thousands of people. As a law enforcement official told a Tamaulipas radio audience, "If the cartels would stop killing each other, there would be enough money for everyone."[252] In somewhat similar fashion, the fervency of

---

252 The laissez faire PRI administrations of the latter half of the twentieth century primarily collected quotas ("rights to operate payments") from the so-called cartels, leaving them to compete among themselves without having to confront government

the anti-immigrant movement in the United States didn't play fair with the tacit agreement between employers and enforcement by complicating the former's easy access to cheap temporary labor. Laws propagated by citizen groups, many sponsored by Tea Party advocates, included employer restrictions and greater federal enforcement.

These restrictions impacted sender communities south of the border, exacerbating unemployment and prompting potential emigrants to merge into criminal organizations. That put the United States in the undesirable situation of funding efforts to curb crime while providing the criminal organizations with increased manpower.

As transporting marijuana and cocaine across the border became more difficult, Mexico ceased to be solely a supplier nation. Drug use in Mexico increased. Breakaway groups from the major drug importing corporations branched into people smuggling, shakedowns, kidnappings, auto theft, and other activities, many of which included collusion by law enforcement and other government officials.

Governments dominated by global capitalism no longer respond to citizens' needs for employment and relief from poverty, but instead focus on controlling the population. In Mexico, this control led to militarization of law enforcement efforts to curb the rising power of the drug corporations. Despite President Calderón's insistence that "it is everyone's duty" to be involved in the war against drugs, the impunity granted the military separated the efforts to combat drug production and exportation from the needs of general populace.

What Calderón seemed to want was blanket approval for the militarization, not citizen participation. The citizenry, devastated by the violence of the drug wars and escalating criminality, sought security through the father-figure, the state, but was rejected by it. Rejected and victimized. As tax money and U.S. aid were diverted to combat organized crime, world financial organizations urged the cutback of social programs.

"This is exactly backward," Laura Carlson insisted. "Strong communities—ones with jobs, ample educational

---

intrusions.

190

opportunities and coverage of basic needs and services–are better able to resist the infiltration of organized crime" than armed intervention by what many residents considered "mercenaries"—Mexican soldiers and marines who had no connections with the people of the areas in which they were stationed.[253]

The government's inability to provide security further prioritized security as a political and social issue. Calderón's U.S.-backed, anti-drug efforts responded by increasing executive authority and quashing social protest.

At the same time, through bribes and quasi-legal procedures, foreign interests—primarily U.S., Canadian, and Spanish—assumed greater roles in Mexico's petroleum and energy producing industries. Canadian mining corporations virtually monopolized gold, silver, and copper exploration and production by acquiring long-term territorial and property rights, often falsifying ecological reports in the process. Affirmations about *apegado a la ley* and ecological adherence were without substance as water and land pollution intensified and agricultural commercialization gave way to importing basic commodities and producing large scale export items.

When Vicente Fox was elected president in 2000, he openly advocated "government of, by and for entrepreneurs." Opening the nationalized petroleum industry to foreign investment was one of his government's announced priorities; although measures to do this were presented to Congress, the administration was able to sidestep anticipated disapproval through processes that only required the industry's governing board's approval. (The board included several of the nation's wealthiest entrepreneurs who had financed Fox's election campaign.).

Co-opted union leaders smoothed the way for these administrative changes by aligning themselves with the entrepreneurs (and in the process acquiring mansions, yachts, aircraft, and foreign bank accounts). The Mexican Congress validated the establishment of non-exclusive unions in various leading industries; owner-instituted syndicates siphoned membership and power away from the

253 Americas Program of the Center for International Policy in Mexico City. *www.cipamericas.org.*

independents. Government prosecutors filed corruption charges against the leaders of several major unions, including the mine workers and electrical workers unions. In 2009, through presidential decree, the federal government dissolved the Central Light and Power Company, leaving its union membership unemployed and without affiliation.[254]

This erosion of union power accompanied a regression in wages and salaries throughout Mexico. Many major industries and business enterprises (particularly those affiliated with transnational corporations) replaced permanent employees with personnel acquired through outsourcing. In many cases, those involved simply replaced themselves but as employment agency workers rather than vested employees.

Declining wages, increased under and unemployment, strangulation of the emigration safety valve and commercialization of communal and *ejido* lands debilitated Mexicans' ability to cope socially and financially. Crime escalated, poverty increased, and the separation between the entrepreneurial/management class and the majority of the population widened. By 2010, the country was regressing into the nineteenth century Mexico of Porfirio Díaz with its small ultra-wealthy aristocracy and huge servile working class.

3

However, 2010 was not 1910. The dangers of explosion pointed northward and the financial crises of 2008-2009 altered relationships between Mexico and the United States. The latter faced its own internal landmines as unemployment and debt increased. Anti-Mexican

---

254 A member of that union in a protest encampment in Mexico City's Zócalo told me in 2010 that nearly half of the Electrical Worker's workforce had "caved in" and accepted government termination pay because "they felt trapped" and put personal material needs above union ideals. Another in the same encampment admitted that the union "wasn't perfect" and the membership had allowed its leaders to profit financially without questioning how dues money was being spent.

sentiments—and politicians responding to them—affected not only temporary migrant workers but also long term residents and second-and third-generation Americans of Mexican descent. This racism and the shriveling of work opportunities impacted millions of Mexican families that depended wholly or in part on remittances from the United States. The result for many was torn loyalties and erosion of their beliefs in and obedience to the two governments.

Who then did one believe in? Not only had federal and regional governments in both nations failed to resolve—or even admit awareness of—the interconnections among what I've termed five landmines, but they seemed unwilling and incapable of doing so. Completing the master plan may still have been a guiding principle in United States-Mexico relations; if so, the process of implementing it evidenced a visible lack of coherence during the first decade of the new century. Immigration policy clashed with—and frequently undermined—drug war policy. Economic insistence on free trade agreements eroded local production and greatly reduced the ability of Mexican consumers to make purchases, debilitating the economy and accelerating undocumented migration and drug organization recruitment.

Privatizations and cuts in federal spending, plus entrepreneurial speculation, exacerbated unemployment and reduced governmental ability to inspect, regulate and contain corruption and violations of environmental agreements. Protests and demonstrations in both countries triggered repression of civil liberties, the rise of vigilante groups and widespread rejection of politics and politicians. The description given by a Chihuahua journalist, "It's like a football game without coaches or referees, soldiers and *narcos* charging this way and that, doing more harm to the spectators than to each other," aptly described inter- and intra-governmental attempts at patching together coherent policy.

That the drug corporations became functioning financial entities elevated them into the world of stock market dealings, international banking, and entrepreneurial investment. The money generated flowed into the economies of both countries—not as something prohibited but as something welcomed. Regulating it—or attempting to regulate it—conflicted with economic gain; consequently, efforts to do so had to be made to seem politically acceptable. Midway through his six-year presidential term, Calderón replaced "war on drugs" rhetoric with "combating organized crime" to make militarization more palatable to a majority of Mexicans. (The United States already had defined its anti-immigrant policies as "securing our frontiers against terrorism.")

Redefining policy to make it publicly acceptable rather than changing it cloaked financial dealings and separated interwoven issues into more easily publicized categories: "combat against crime," "securing our borders," "regulating immigration," "free trade," "caring for the environment." As gaps between word and deed widened, the landmines became more volatile and distrust of government motives increased. Band-Aids and publicity photos ceased to have the desired effects.

4

Is it possible to navigate the minefield without setting off an explosion? (Or better yet, defuse the landmines before they explode?)

There is no obvious answer. Nor solution. World War II landmines lay dormant for decades; others were set off by animals, by children, by construction equipment long after hostilities had ceased. The issues affecting Mexico and the United States are interconnected, and events beyond the boundaries of the two countries, particularly precarious economic circumstances, come into play. From the statements being made and the actions taken by those responsible for dictating and implementing decisions concerning these interconnections, one has to presume that a great deal remains *debajo el agua*, undetected and not discussed.

How well—or whether—legislators and bureaucrats understand (or attempt to understand) these interconnections arouses doubts. Lawmakers respond to those who vote for them and those who finance their campaigns—often the two don't coincide. Almost invariably, legislators find it easier to deal with symptoms rather than causes.

To summarize:

Migration/Immigration:

1. In 2008, approximately eleven million four-hundred thousand undocumented immigrants were employed full or nearly full-time in the United States, i.e. the jobs were there and apparently not difficult to secure.

2. Dependents of emigrant workers, legal and undocumented, sent twenty-four billion dollars to Mexican residents, income that rivaled the proceeds from oil revenues and drug sales.

3. The availability of inexpensive labor benefitted U.S. employers, and the money earned enabled the Mexican government to cut back social spending.

4. Protests against the presence of undocumented immigrants and the continued influx of new arrivals triggered social discontent that the U.S. government attempted to mollify by focusing on increasing enforcement of immigration regulations. (The Mexican government did the same with regard to Central American immigrants entering that country.)

5. Prosecuting symptoms, not causes, benefitted the status quo: cheap labor for employers, remittances for Mexican families, jobs for millions of workers despite the risks of deportation and discrimination, and outlets for discontent that otherwise might have been directed towards the government or private enterprise.

6. Exacerbated by the world financial crisis of 2008-2009, protests increased, deportations and incarcerations increased, unemployment increased, which resulted in greater poverty and criminal activity.

War on Drugs

1. Drug-exporting organizations—now full-fledged transnational corporations—grew exponentially and accrued immense wealth, prompting break-off

groups to compete and to branch into other criminal activities.

2. Drug use and the market for drugs in the United States decreased only slightly. The U.S. government made only token attempts to reduce the demand. No matter how many drug corporation *capos* were arrested or slain, new suppliers competed to fulfill that demand.

3. The continued prohibition—illegality—of narcotics commerce engendered guerrilla warfare, which by 2010 had taken 50,000 lives, caused thousands of disappearances, the destruction of cities and ranchos, and the recruitment of hundreds of thousands of new participants.

4. Drug use in Mexico escalated as exportation became more difficult and cocaine and marijuana became more accessible and less expensive locally.

5. The wealth generated by commerce in narcotics enabled drug corporations to co-opt law enforcement, including high-ranking military and political figures.

6. Mexico's federal government dramatically increased military and law enforcement spending and drastically reducing expenditures for social services, education, and health.

Popular Protest

1. Privatizations encouraged by international lending organizations triggered the replacement of permanent employees with outsourced temporaries, the breaking up of labor unions, and an unequal distribution of wealth.

2. Riot police quelled anti-government demonstrations, particularly those in Oaxaca, the Estado de Mexico, and Guerrero. Numerous protest leaders were assassinated; others were arrested and jailed.

3. Propaganda campaigns and superficial endorsement of international human rights treaties veiled the inefficiency of the judicial system and failures to apply existent laws.

4. The television duopoly's interaction with (if not control of) the federal government distorted events

and the problems that nurtured them. Government became a "reality show" that bore little or no resemblance to actuality.

Corruption

1. As politicians' accessibility to wealth increased, concern for basic issues like poverty, the ecology, technological advancement, education, and health decreased. The gap between those in power—the elite—and the dwindling middle-class, working class, and rural and urban poor widened dramatically.

2. Foreign corporations and governments willingly participated in the bribery of public officials, "good ol' boy" payoffs, and abrogation of financial and environmental laws.

3. Over half-a-century of interconnections between drug corporations and public officials, particularly those involved in law enforcement and the customs service, debilitated efforts to combat narcotics production and export.

4. Public perception of corruption in law enforcement, the congresses, and the executive branches of federal and state governments engendered a "follow the leader" attitude towards illegal and immoral financial and social dealings. ("If they do it why shouldn't I?")

5. Fraudulent electoral practices, including payoffs to voters, abuses of campaign laws, and the filling of cabinet seats and other government positions with supporters and friends seriously weakened the government's ability to function effectively and honestly.

Ecology

1. Emphasis on producing raw materials for export, principally petroleum but also minerals and lumber, rather than developing infrastructure and local production negatively impacted agriculture and increased the demand for imported goods.

2. Lack of effective regulations and enforcement of environmental norms permitted oil and mineral

exploitation to contaminate rivers, lakes, and urban water tables.

3. Persistent droughts crimped agriculture, particularly in the northern and central states, reducing farm production and prompting hundreds of thousands of small landholders to emigrate.

4. Diversion of funds earmarked for environmental protection nullified laws designed for that purpose.

5. Fraudulent approval of huge developmental projects, including tourism, mining, and timber harvesting, reduced claims of environmental protection to simulation, not compliance. Antiquated waste disposal systems and diversion of water supplies to industry and tourist developments exacerbated drought damage and contaminated water tables.

None of these land-mined areas existed separately. Attempting to isolate and resolve one problem exacerbated the others. The refusals, or inabilities, to create a comprehensive view—understanding—of the interconnections stalemated actions to relieve one or another and left governing powers on both sides of the frontier with lessened authority and lessened control.

Effectively diffusing the landmines—a long and tedious labor—demands a comprehensive overview, rather than a sequence of disconnected actions. It necessitates acknowledging that protectionism in the form of militarizing the War on Drugs and militarizing campaigns against undocumented immigration conflicts with free market, free trade philosophy. Even if one acknowledges that commerce in narcotics and undocumented immigration dirties the free market flow, one has to realize that obstructing that flow by constructing dams (walls—steel, barbed wire, electronic) doesn't enable one to clean the water. Instead, the water backs up, forming pestilent cesspools that breed criminality and violence.

To clean the water one has to go to the source of the contamination. In the case of narcotics commerce, the source is the unabated market for cocaine, marijuana, and designer drugs that exists worldwide but specifically in the United States. As long as this market exists and does not significantly diminish, militarized violence only ups the stakes; the more risky the commerce becomes, the more rewarding the economic returns, and the more violent the competition to provide the market with its desired products.

In the case of undocumented immigration, the source is poverty and the inequality of wealth in Mexico and the need for cheap labor in the United States. As long as 60 percent of Mexico's citizenry falls beneath the poverty level —20 percent in extreme poverty—emigration will continue. And as long as U.S. agriculture, business, and service industries need affordable labor, the hiring of *indocumentados* will continue. Militarized repression ups the stakes; violence increases and with it greater criminality.

The solutions attempted during the first decade of the twenty-first century cost tens of thousands of lives without ending commerce in narcotics (which had been going on for over a century) and without ending undocumented immigration (which had been going on for over a century). Widespread poverty south of the border is an impetus for migration, a trigger for criminal activity, and the root of social protest. It feeds corruption, negates environmental protection, and invalidates education. A poverty riddled Mexico is itself a landmine that cannot remain unexploded indefinitely.

Arresting and deporting undocumented immigrants exacerbates the reality of poverty that envelopes millions of Mexican citizens. Those deported lack homes, jobs, places in society; they are forced to risk their lives by emigrating again or risk their lives by trying to take criminally what they can't obtain legally. Lacking the safety valve of emigration, the 700,000-1 million young people thrust into what should be the work force every year face a situation many of them view as hopeless ("better to die young and with something than old and without anything"). As long as deportation-exacerbated poverty exists, crime—especially drug commerce—will flourish.

Pursuit of and combat against drug organization *capos* and militants changes the makeup of those organizations and impedes their ability to function, but does not alter the demand for the product. As long as the demand exists—and the wealth to be gained for meeting that demand exists —new *capos* will move in, new recruits replace those killed or incapacitated. The billions spent to deter them makes their activity more dangerous; consequently, they militarize their own operations. This militarization increases death tolls and violence rather than reducing it.

By 2010, governmental-acknowledged poverty rates had risen to nearly 50 percent in Mexico and nearly 15 percent in the United States. Anti-immigrant legislation and stricter border control efforts made entering the United States more difficult and more hazardous for Mexican jobseekers but only slightly reduced undocumented immigration and the demand for undocumented workers. Unemployment in both countries increased and with it anti-government, anti-financial institution, and anti-immigrant protests and violence. Rising crime rates in both countries accompanied the rising unemployment and poverty rates.

Corporate control of the media in both countries deformed and eroded news coverage and analysis, enabling government and financial institution-backed entrepreneurs to whitewash corrupt ecological and business practices and the inefficiency of militarization to control drug exportation. Wikileaks disclosures undermined confidence in the government in both countries, and the popularity of Facebook and Twitter gave voice to discontent in both Mexico and the United States.

By 2010, the two countries were perched on the brink of change. Governmental and entrepreneurial forces that had been acting to defend the problematical status quo were being pushed by popular discontent to change policies, not simply the names and faces of those elected or promoted to leadership positions. In their reluctance—or inability—to change, those in power refused to consider that what they were doing was not working. More than that, what they could have done was focused on repression and assumptions that "government" consisted only of those involved in governing and not those who were governed.

The War on Drugs is a prime example. The U.S. supported militarization created a situation where an invading army was battling a guerrilla force in its own territory—a territory it knew intimately and in which by allegiance or force it controlled the civilian population. Although the army was Mexican, operating in Mexican territory, its membership was not local. To the people of Tamaulipas, of Sinaloa, of Oaxaca the soldiers were foreigners, no better and no less hostile and no less violent than the drug organizations' criminal bands.

As viewed by Washington, and by Calderòn's government, the War on Drugs was a battle between two armies, and the civilian population didn't exist. (Deaths, rapes, disappearances, destruction of personal property were "collateral," i.e. incidentals not to be taken into account, "mere nothings" in the words of a Ciudad Juàrez mother whose sons disappeared after a military incursion.) One might suppose that the U.S. had learned from Vietnam—and from Iraq and Afghanistan—that guerrilla warfare cannot be won by nineteenth century army versus army alignments on designated battlefields. But the U.S. government's promotion of the militarization of the War on Drugs belied any such learning.

President Calderòn's belated appeal that "the fight against organized crime is everybody's job," though potentially true, lacked credibility. What Calderòn was saying, in essence, was, "I am the commander-in-chief so everybody support me," i.e. accept without question or dissent or there will be deaths, destruction, and disappearances. The U.S. government underpublicized the effects of the "war" it had engineered, permitted (and in some cases actually originated) the flow of arms to the drug corporations, and lauded the achievements of Mexico's president Calderòn (who U.S. President Barack Obama described as "my Eliot Ness").

By shunting aside the majority of citizens as "mere nothings," the United States/Mexico's War on Drugs lost what should have been their great ally. If, as some estimates indicated, a million citizens were somehow involved in the illegal commerce in narcotics, 100 million were not. Neither were they enlisted or utilized as an anti-criminal force. By contrast, the major drug organizations hired thousands of lookouts, scouts, mechanics, cooks, messengers, bankers, police, mayors, truck drivers, and congresspersons. Very much like the Viet Cong during 1965-1977, they became the resident power. Their tentacles infiltrated every aspect of community life, whereas the foreign armed force did not.

Had the two governments dedicated themselves to enlisting and providing citizen support including education, surveillance, local militia, and investigating and weeding out corruption, and had they sponsored community designed construction projects and supported local agriculture, they could have built barriers to the territorial and financial expansion of the drug corporations and greatly limited their operating power. A strengthened citizenry could have fortified investigation and prosecution of corruption in both the private and governmental sections rather than having been increasingly victimized.

Any first-year economics student at a public university could have drafted a plan to unite the demand for inexpensive labor with the availability of an immigrant work force. If 96 percent of twelve million *indocumentados* were holding down paying jobs, then a demand—a need—for labor certainly existed. On the left side of the page, list the demand, on the right side, the supply and work out ways to bring the two together. Obviously mechanisms would have to be created to make the resolutions function, there would be trial and error and some dissatisfactions and revisions, but workable solutions would be possible. The least workable—one that the beginning economics student wouldn't even consider—would be to criminalize both sides of the equation and spent billions of dollars building walls and prisons and militarizing the frontier.

That a high percentage of financial dealings by both government and private enterprise were conducted *debajo el agua* further separated the coteries of power from the majority of citizens of both countries. Government/private enterprise collusion facilitated transfers of billions in narcotics sales from bank to bank to financial havens, turned over hundreds of thousands of hectares of communal lands to mining operations, deferred or returned tax payments, facilitated an unrestricted flow of armaments, penetrated telephone and electronic correspondence, and enriched thousands of politicians and entrepreneurs at the expense of those who were governed.

As corruption increased and the economy bottomed out, consumer spending decreased. The removal of subsidies drove the costs of basic necessities like propane, gasoline, electricity, transportation, and education higher. Speculation and corrupt marketing practices that created artificial food shortages doubled and tripled the consumer price of basic food products including corn, eggs, and milk. Profit taking supplanted customer service. Banking speculation replaced investment and consumer loans. Free market philosophy floundered as unemployment, under-employment, layoffs, and small business collapses eroded the consumer base. The lack of transparency in financial dealings, including those permitted among drug corporations, government officials, and private investors turned attempts to resolve major problems—drug commerce, undocumented immigration, ecological devastation—into mere tinkering—tinkering that vitally affected the majority of citizens but excluded them from participation. Or forced them to participate as outsiders banging on the doors for admittance.

The banging increased dramatically from 2000 to 2010. Massive protests, stimulated in part by communications technology, demonstrated how incapable governments had become to identify and resolve this complex of interlocked circumstances. Drug consumption, employment, poverty, corruption, the environment are people issues; when people no longer are the government, the latter becomes a mere struggle for power that is rendered less and less effective. Incapable of resolving issues, those who govern retreat into veiling these problems with media hype, showmanship, and vacuous promises.

Not that solutions are easy. They aren't. But segmenting in order to simplify—or in order to please certain sectors of the populace (focusing on symptoms, not causes)—compounds the disease; it worsens, and the symptoms become more severe.

Recognition—accurate and politically unbiased evaluation of how these symptoms are interconnected—is necessary. The following decisions over drug use have to be made: Given the demand, what responsibilities do governments have? What do a majority of citizens want and what are pro- and anti-groups willing to accept? How has militarization—the War on Drugs—affected criminality, and why has militarization not been effective?

By the same token, how has deportation and discrimination affected undocumented immigration, and what links exist between criminalizing unauthorized entry and increased criminal activities and violence? How do employers of the over ten million undocumented workers in the United States benefit from the availability of (persecuted) undocumented emigrant workers? How does Mexico benefit from having over 10 percent of its population living and working in the United States?

How do financial and entrepreneurial enterprises benefit from the money generated by drug sales? How do they benefit—and how do governments benefit—from ecologically damaging industrial and agricultural developments? How do they benefit from the growing inequality of wealth distribution? How do they deal with social and political protest? What role does the media play in controlling public opinion and disguising reality? How long can that control last?

The answers are not theoretical; they derive going past the symptoms to interconnected issues that are the causes of the maladies and recognizing how well or how badly individual treatments have affected these causes. Just as in medicine, there is no permanent solution; however, lasting improvement can be achieved by honestly evaluating the disease and its causes and basing treatment on those evaluations.

Or one by one—or altogether—the landmines can explode.

BIBLIOGRAPHY

Books and Documents

Astorga, Luis. *El siglo de las drogas.* Mexico City: Random House-Mondadori, 2005.

Beas, Carlos. *La batalla por Oaxaca.* Oaxaca: Ediciones Yope Power, 2007.

Bellinghausen, Hermann. *Acteal, crimen de estado.* Mexico, D. F.: La Jornada Books, 2008.

Blanco, José Joaquín. *Un chavo bien helado.* Mexico, Ediciones Era, 1990.

Chomsky, Noam, and David Barsamian. *In What We Say Goes: Conversations on U.S. Power in a Changing World.* New York: Metropolitan Books, 2007.

Campbell, Federico. *La invención del poder.* Mexico, D. F.: Aguilar, Altea, Taurus, Alfaguara, 2001.

Clouthier, Tatiana. *Maquío, mi padre.* Mexico, D. F.: Random House Mondadori, 2007.

Cruz, Francisco. *El cártel de Juárez.* Mexico, D. F.: Planeta Temas de Hoy, 2008.

Cruz, José Antonio. *Absalón Castellanos y los terratenientes.* Universidad Autónoma de Chiapas, 1982.

Codevilla, Ugo. *2006-2009, La Coyuntura Adversa.* Mexico, D. F.: Miguel Ángel Porrúa, 2008.

Denham, Diana (ed). *Teaching Rebellion*, Oakland, California.: PM Press, 2008.

Galarza, Ernesto. *Merchants of Labor: the Mexican Bracero Story.* Santa Barbara: McNally and Loftin, 1964.

Granados-Chapa, Miguel Àngel. *Fox & Co.* Mexico D. F.: Grijalbo, 2000.

Greenwood, Michael J., and Marta Tienda. "U.S. Impacts on Mexican Migration." Austin: University of Texas Press, 1998.

Gutièrrez-Vivo, José, coordinador. *El mexicano y su siglo.* Editorial Oceano de Mexico, 1999.

Korrodi, Lino. *Me la jugué.* Grijalbo, 2003.

Lelo de Larrea, Francisco, in Rodarte, Mario E., ed. La economía política del maíz en Mèxico. Mexico, D. F.: Centro de Estudios Econòmicos del Sector Privado A.C., 2007.

Loret de Mola, Rafael. *Destapes.* Oceano, 2004.

Marcos, Subcomandante Insurgente. *The Speed of Dreams.* Edited by Canek Peña-Vargas. San Francisco: Greg Ruggiero, City Lights, 2007.

Martìnez-Vàsquez, Vìctor Raùl (coordinador). *La APPO: rebelión o Oaxaca, movimiento social?.* Universidad Autònoma "Benito Juàrez" de Oaxaca, 2009.

Massey, Douglas S., Jorge Durand, and Nolan J. Malone. *Beyond Smoke and Mirrors.* New York: Sage, 2002.

Moncada, Jorge Francisco and Mario Alberto Di Costanzo. *El saqueo a los mexicanos.* Mexico, D. F.: Random House Mondadodi, 2005.

"National Project for the Defense of Salary and Employment." Center for Labor Action and Assessment (Cilas). Mexican Electricians Union, 2007.

Nevins, Joseph. *Dying To Live.* San Francisco: City Lights Books, 2008.

Osorno, Diego. *Oaxaca sitiada.* Mexico, D. F.: Random House Mondadora, 2007.

Paris-Pombo, María Dolores. *Oligarquía tradición y ruptura.* Mexico: La Jornada Ediciones, 2001.

Pew Hispanic Center reports, www.pewhispanic.org, 2006.

Ramirez-Marcial, Neptali, Angèlica Camacho-Cruz, and Mario Gonzàlez-Espinosa. *Guìa por la propagaciòn especies leñosas de las altas y Mexico, montañas del Norte de Chiapas.* Colegio de la Frontera Sur, Tapachula, n.d.

Ravelo, Ricardo. *Herencia maldita.* Mexico, D. F.: Random House Mondadori, 2007.

Riding, Alan. *Distant Neighbors.* New York: Vintage Books, 1989.

Romo-Gutiérrez, Arturo. *Última frontera.* Mexico, D. F.: Siglo xxi Editores, 2003.

Scherer, Julio. *Los presidentes.* Mexico, D. F.: Random House Mondadori, 2007.

Scherer-García, Julio and Carlos Monsiváis. *Tiempo de saber.* Mexico, D. F.: Aguilar, 2003.

Semo, Enrique. *La búsqueda.* Mexico, D. F.: Oceano, 2003.

Spykman, Nicholas J. *America's Strategy in World Policy.* New York: Harcourt Brace, 1942.

Stout, Robert Joe. *Why Immigrants Come to America: Braceros, Indocumentados and the Migra,* New York: Praeger, 2008.

Trueba Lara, José Luis. *Los primeros en morir.* Mexico: Nueva Imagen, 1996.

United Nations Development Program, Third Report of the Human Development Index, June 2007.

United States Department of State "Visa Bulletin," August 2006.

U.S. Joint Forces Command. "Joint Operating Environment." November 25, 2008.

Urban Institute. "Undocumented Immigrants: Facts and Figures." January 12, 2004.

Urban Institute, http://www.urban.org/publications/900965 html, 2006.

Verea, Monica. *Entre México y Estados Unidos: los indocumentados.* Mexico, D. F.: Ediciones El Cabellito, 1982.

Villamil, Jenaro. *Si yo fuera presidente. El reality show de Pena Nieto.* Mexico, D. F.: Grijalva, 2009.

Zepeda-Patterson, Jorge. *Los amos de Mexico.* Mexico, D. F.: Ediciones Temas de Hoy, 2007.

Journals, Forums and Online Resources

Aristegui, Carmen. "Reporte Indigo." www.reporteindigo.com.

Bricker, Kristin. mywordismyweapon.blogsport.com.

Bustamante, Jorge A. bibliojuridicas.unam.mx/estrev/pdf/derint/cont/4/se/rse20.pdf.

Carlsen, Laura. "Drug War Doublespeak." Center for International Policy, March 9, 2009.

Centro de Estudios Economicos del Sector Privado, July 2007.

Confederación de Cámaras Nacionales de Comercio Servicios y Turismo (Concanaco) www.concanaco.com.mx.

Cornelius, Wayne A. "Death at the Border: Efficacy and Unintended Consequences of U.S. Immigration Control Policy." *Population and Development Review* 669, 2001.

Consejo Nacional de Poblaciòn, www.conapo.gob.mx.

Diario Oficial de la Federaciòn, www.dof.gob.mx

El pez por su boca muere, www.gurupolitico.com

Garavito, Rosa Albina. "El Articulo 123 y la deuda con las trabajadores en el siglo XXI." forum in Mexico, D.F., January 28, 2011.

Human Rights Watch. http://www.hrw.org/by-issue/publications/72.

Hernández, Anabel. interviewed by Carmen Arestegui on "Reporte Indigo." January 13, 2012.

Miller, Todd. "Is a Social Explosion in the Wings?" NACLA, September 29, 2009.

Instituto Nacional de Antropología y Historia.www.estudioshistoricos.inah.gob.mx/.../histori as_29_121-130.pdf.

Mosca, Gaetano. Glosario De Conceptos Políticos Usuales. http://www.eumed.net.

National Network for Immigrant and Refugee Rights. "Over Raided, Under Siege." January 2008.

Paterson, Kent. "Mexico's New Dirty War." http://americas.irc-online.org/am/6714, April 5, 2010.

Rodríguez-Araujo. Octavio. http://rodriguezaraujo.unam.mx.

Stout, Robert Joe. "A Dónde Mexico?" America. February 22, 2010.

Stout, Robert Joe. "Desmadre." Global Politics. spring 2008.

Stout, Robert Joe. "Do the United States and Mexico Really Want To Win the War on Drugs?" The Monthly Review. January 2012.

Stout, Robert Joe. "'We Want To Be Heard.'" New Politics. winter 2011.

Zafra, Gloria, and Magdalen López-Rocha. "Impacto de la Migración en el papel de las mujeres en el ámbito publico." Centro de Estudios para el Desarrollo Rural y la Soberania Alementaria, 2005.

Zepeda-Patterson. Jorge www.jorgezepeda.net.

Periodicals (print and electronic)

Arkansas Democrat-Gazette

Al Jazeera

Associated Press

Cimacnoticias

Ciudad Juárez *Ahora*

Contralinea

El Paso *Times*

Expat Chronicles

Fox *News Latino*

Mexico, D.F. *La Jornada*

Mexico, D. F. *El Milenio*

Mexico, D.F. *El Universal*

Mexico, D.F. *Excélsior*

Mexico, D.F. *Ultimas Noticias*

Mexico Labor News and Analysis

Narco News

New York *Times*

Oaxaca, Mexico *Noticias, Voz e Imagen de Oaxaca*

Proceso

Viva

Yahoo! Voices